101 THINGS YOU DIDN'T KNOW ABOUT

Jane Austen

101 THINGS YOU DIDN'T KNOW ABOUT

Jane Austen

The Truth about the World's Most Intriguing Romantic Literary Heroine

PATRICE HANNON, Ph.D.

Adams Media

Avon, Massachusetts

Copyright © 2007, F+W Publications, Inc.
All rights reserved.
This book, or parts thereof, may not be reproduced in any
form without permission from the publisher; exceptions
are made for brief excerpts used in published reviews.

Published by Adams Media, an F+W Publications Company
57 Littlefield Street, Avon, MA 02322
www.adamsmedia.com.

ISBN 10: 1-59869-284-4
ISBN 13: 978-1-59869-284-6

Printed in Canada.

J I H G F E D C B

Library of Congress Cataloging-in-Publication Data
is available from the publisher.

This publication is designed to provide accurate and authoritative information with regard to
the subject matter covered. It is sold with the understanding that the publisher is not engaged
in rendering legal, accounting, or other professional advice. If legal advice or other expert assistance is required, the services of a competent professional person should be sought.
—From a *Declaration of Principles* jointly adopted by a Committee of the
American Bar Association and a Committee of Publishers and Associations

Many of the designations used by manufacturers and sellers to distinguish their products are
claimed as trademarks. Where those designations appear in this book and Adams Media was
aware of a trademark claim, the designations have been printed with initial capital letters.

*This book is available at quantity discounts for bulk purchases.
For information, please call 1-800-289-0963.*

For Aunt Jean, and in loving memory of Uncle Dan,
Uncle Frank, and Aunt Dorothy.

Acknowledgments

As always, I would like to thank my family, my friends, and my students for their love and support. I would like to give special thanks to Paula Munier, Brendan O'Neill, Kate Petrella, and Andrea Norville, all at Adams Media, and to Margaret Sullivan and Kerri Spennicchia.

About the Author

Patrice Hannon holds a Ph.D. in English literature from Rutgers University. She is the author of *Dear Jane Austen: A Heroine's Guide to Life and Love*. Originally from New Jersey, she now lives in New York.

For Aunt Jean, and in loving memory of Uncle Dan,
Uncle Frank, and Aunt Dorothy.

Acknowledgments

As always, I would like to thank my family, my friends, and my students for their love and support. I would like to give special thanks to Paula Munier, Brendan O'Neill, Kate Petrella, and Andrea Norville, all at Adams Media, and to Margaret Sullivan and Kerri Spennicchia.

About the Author

Patrice Hannon holds a Ph.D. in English literature from Rutgers University. She is the author of *Dear Jane Austen: A Heroine's Guide to Life and Love*. Originally from New Jersey, she now lives in New York.

Contents

Part 4: The Glorious Years 84

Part 5: Heroes and Heroines 134

Part 7: Austen and Popular Culture: From the Eighteenth Century to the Twenty-First....217

Introduction

In the "Biographical Notice of the Author" that was published with two of Jane Austen's novels after her death, Henry Austen said that his sister's "was not by any means a life of event." For a long time this was the popular view of Jane Austen—as a genteel old maid, removed from the hurly-burly of the great world. In recent years we have seen a reconsideration and a revision of this position. The greatest novelist who ever lived in fact saw—at close range—and experienced quite a lot in her too-short life. She was touched by crime, imprisonment, execution, bankruptcy, early and tragic death (again and again), broken engagements, and, on the happier side, deep love and great admiration. In this book we shall see how 101 aspects of Jane Austen contributed to the creation of the most perceptive and enjoyable novels ever written: *Northanger Abbey*, *Sense and Sensibility*, *Pride and Prejudice*, *Mansfield Park*, *Emma*, and *Persuasion*. Additionally, we shall explore many wonderful shorter pieces by Austen that most people don't even know about.

What makes Elizabeth Bennet, Emma Woodhouse, and their sister heroines so endlessly fascinating? Some clues can be found in the fascinating life of their creator!

PART I

Birth of a Heroine

1 THE AUSTENS OF STEVENTON

Can anything in Jane Austen's family background account for her literary genius? She was born at home in the Steventon parsonage, Hampshire, England, on December 16, 1775, the seventh child of the Reverend George Austen and his wife, Cassandra (née Leigh). One more child would follow Jane three and a half years later—a boy. Jane would then have six brothers and just one sister, the beloved Cassandra. The large family lived on a clergyman's small salary supplemented by earnings from the boys' school run by Mr. and Mrs. Austen. The rectory was also a working farm, with fields of crops, a dairy, and a poultry yard. In a child-rearing arrangement quite different from our own, the Austen children were sent to foster mothers (possibly wet nurses) in the village a few months after birth and then returned to the parsonage after around a year or eighteen months. The Austens certainly didn't neglect the children they sent away: They visited them daily when possible. It may seem odd—and cold—to us, but attitudes toward children were different then, and the Austens were in fact very loving parents.

In addition to the two girls, Cassandra and Jane, there were the six Austen boys: James, George, Edward, Henry, Francis (known as Frank), and Charles. The second son, George (named after his father), was the only one who never returned from his foster family. He suffered from some kind of affliction—we do not know exactly what sort—and did not develop normally. He is not much discussed in family documents—at least not in the ones that have survived—but he was well cared for in the Hampshire village of Monk Sherborne along with Mrs. Austen's brother Thomas, who also was unable to care for himself, and George lived to the good age of seventy-two.

The other children were healthy and bright (to say the least!) and the parsonage must have been a lively place when the whole family was there together. Although nothing in this picture can explain Austen's genius, we can find traces of her early life in the parsonage throughout her writings. We see in the novels just how important family life is to Austen, and how parents and siblings have such a powerful influence on her young heroines, whether for good or evil, happiness or misery. We see also the deep attachment some of those heroines have to the place they call home. But even after their time with their foster families had ended, the two little Austen girls, to their sorrow, did not always live at home in the cherished company of their parents and brothers, and some of Austen's heroines also feel the pain of enforced separation from home. Where did Jane and Cassandra go? We will find out where they were sent, and why.

2 BLOODLINE OF A GENIUS

What was Jane Austen's lineage? On her mother's side it was somewhat grand, at least if you take into account the extended family—as her mother certainly did. Mrs. Austen was very proud of her high connections. She was born Cassandra Leigh, and many of the Leighs had become nobility themselves or married into the aristocracy. Moreover, her uncle Theophilus Leigh held the esteemed position of Master of Balliol College at Oxford University. Mrs. Austen was certainly clever enough herself to justify a suspicion that Jane's intellect was the greatest manifestation of a Leigh trait.

Jane Austen's uncle James inherited a fortune from a different uncle—not Theophilus—and would therefore change his name to Leigh-Perrot. (As we will see, such name changes occur with some frequency in Austen's family.) Jane's maternal grandfather was, less grandly, the parish priest in the village of Harpsden.

One of Mrs. Austen's relations was the owner of Stoneleigh Abbey, a large estate in Warwickshire on the beautiful banks of the Avon. In 1806 Mrs. Austen would take Jane and Cassandra there while on a round of visits to cousins. Mrs. Austen wrote glowingly of the place to her daughter-in-law Mary back at Steventon, and her letter contains just the sort of joke that might have come from Jane herself. The house is so grand and the hallways such a maze that Mrs. Austen declares, "I have proposed his setting up *directing Posts* at the angles." That combination of dryness and silliness is pure Austen!

George Austen, Jane's father, was orphaned young and had no such ties to the aristocracy, but he did have a very rich uncle, Francis Austen, who assisted him financially. George was intelligent and hardworking, attending St. John's College, Oxford, on a scholarship. He was ordained a priest in the Church of England at the age of twenty-four. The Reverend Austen returned to St. John's to be an assistant chaplain, and was soon to be known there as "the handsome Proctor." He married Cassandra Leigh on April 26, 1764, at the old church of St. Swithin in Bath. Before moving into the rectory at Steventon, where Jane would be born, the pair set up housekeeping in the parsonage of the neighboring parish of Deane, where Mr. Austen would also later become rector.

As the evidence of their large family of intelligent, ambitious, and ultimately successful children shows, Jane Austen's parents did an extraordinary job of bringing up children in that modest rectory. As for her mother's noble blood—well, we shall see how the subject of nobility is treated in Austen's novels.

3 LATE-EIGHTEENTH-CENTURY ENGLAND: AUSTEN AND REVOLUTION

Jane Austen is usually called a nineteenth-century writer, and with good reason: Her novels were either written or revised—and they were all first published—in that century. But most of her life (twenty-five of forty-one years) was lived in the prior century, and the events and literature of that time are so influential in her work that we might be justified in calling her an eighteenth-century writer as well. So what was the last quarter of that century in England like? The world of Austen's youth witnessed two of the most significant events in history: the American and French Revolutions, beginning in, of course, 1775 and 1789. England, we might note, managed to avoid a revolution of its own, but it felt the effects of the revolutionary tide: There were riots and other expressions of discontent with the status quo and of sympathy with the radical sentiments.

As we shall see, the violence of the French Revolution would hit close to home for the Austens. With Jane's brothers Frank and Charles in the Royal Navy and Henry in the Oxford Militia, England's war with France in the 1790s would strike even closer, making world affairs the direct, heartfelt concern of the family. Cassandra Austen would be devastated by her fiancé's participation in that war.

Few periods of history are as fascinating to most people today as the Napoleonic era. As Caroline Austen wrote of her aunt Jane, "Anyone *might* naturally desire to know what part such a mind as her's had taken in the great strifes of war and policy which so disquieted Europe for more than 20 years." And yet, she continues, "In vain do I try to recall any word or expression of Aunt Jane's that had reference to public events." Caroline's brother James-Edward writes of their aunt: "The politics of the day occupied very little of her attention, but she probably shared the feeling of moderate Toryism which prevailed in her family."

Still, some elements of war and other political matters turn up in the novels. Soldiers and sailors certainly make their appearances and even discuss their military duties. Mr. Wickham and his fellow militia officers play an important role in *Pride and Prejudice*. Additionally, in *Persuasion*, a comparison is made between men of old and new orders, and Austen's sympathy is clearly on just one side—that of the largely self-made sailors rather than the privileged aristocracy—so perhaps we can infer some political commentary there. Austen does comment explicitly on the behavior of England's Prince Regent in her letters.

But how important are world affairs overall in Austen's writings? Many twentieth-century critics made much of the mention of slavery in several places in her books because of the seemingly overt political nature of those references. Austen's attitude toward the French Revolution also has been debated. But the fact is that though political and military matters make appearances in her writing, Austen's primary concern is not with them. The political themes of the wider world—including revolution and liberation—show up in the novels as they relate in particular situations to women and marriage, women and work, women and independence, women and money—but they have been very much refined and domesticated.

We do not read Austen to learn about political history. In fact, her novels could not be further from the "real solemn history" Catherine Morland, the heroine of *Northanger Abbey*, finds so dreary: "The quarrels of popes and kings, with wars or pestilences, in every page; the men all so good for nothing, and hardly any women at all; it is very tiresome." Austen's interest lies, rather, in creating new worlds with dazzling language, drawing her inspiration not from wars and pestilences but from—as she puts it so nicely in *Emma*—"all those little matters on which the daily happiness of private life depends."

4 BEAUTIFUL HAMPSHIRE

With all her intellectual sophistication and a satirical wit that would have shone in the most urbane of London salons, and despite the pleasure she found in visiting London and other cities, Jane Austen was at heart a country girl. She deeply loved the Hampshire countryside where she grew up, and she was overjoyed to return to the country once again in later life. Like her heroines, she was a great walker, and country walking is much more pleasant exercise than city walking—at least when the roads are dry. When the roads were wet, the Austen girls wore "pattens"—inelegant but practical overshoes designed to keep the feet dry on sloppy roads. Austen's pleasure in this activity calls to mind *Pride and Prejudice*, in which Elizabeth Bennet, another witty country girl, walks alone to Netherfield, "jumping over stiles and springing over puddles with impatient activity, and finding herself at last within view of the house, with weary ancles, dirty stockings, and a face glowing with the warmth of exercise."

The Steventon rectory was, after all, a farm, with all the elements of one. Jane must have been particularly familiar with her mother's domain: the garden, dairy, and poultry yard. Indeed, her letters and novels reveal an intimate acquaintance with the natural world, and with the pleasures and inconveniences of each season in the country.

The society around Steventon also afforded Jane great pleasure, and her novels are focused on country rather than town society. As she very famously wrote to her niece Anna, who was writing a novel herself, "You are now collecting your People delightfully, getting them exactly into such a spot as is the delight of my life;—3 or 4 Families in a Country Village is the very thing to work on."

Yes, Jane Austen loved Hampshire, and the county now returns the favor: She is its favorite child, and the places significant in her life are venerated. Interestingly, however, Austen did not actually set her novels in rural Hampshire (although the town of Portsmouth appears in a most unflattering light in *Mansfield Park*). The place that was everything in her life does not appear—at least not undisguised—in her art.

5 A FAMILY MEMBER MEETS THE GUILLOTINE

Betsy Hancock was the daughter of Mr. Austen's sister Philadelphia and her husband, Tysoe Saul Hancock. She was fourteen years older than her cousin Jane, in whose life she would play a very large role, particularly from 1797 on. But that part of the story will be told later. Eliza, as she later chose to be called, had a fascinating life even before that time—one that passed far beyond the limited geographic boundaries of her famous cousin's life.

Betsy was born in India in 1761. Her mother had gone there nine years earlier, as many young women did at the time, to improve her chances of finding a well-to-do husband. There is some speculation that Hancock was not the father and that Phila had been having an affair with the prominent trader and civil servant (later to be Governor-General) Warren Hastings. The truth is not known in this matter, but Hastings would take a lifelong interest in his godchild Betsy, conferring a large gift of money upon her after the death of Hancock. (And, in a strange turn of events, Hastings's only son, George, would die while under the care of the Austens.) Already we see that Eliza's life was not quite run-of-the-mill!

Eliza and her widowed mother lived abroad, staying for a time in Paris, where she moved in the highest circles—so much so that she was able to describe Marie Antoinette's outrageously opulent Turkish dress at a ball. At the age of nineteen she married a handsome French officer named Jean François Capot de Feuillide, a captain in the Queen's regiment. He was not in fact a member of the nobility, although Eliza would claim for him the title of "count" and for herself, naturally, "countess." Although not nobility, Jean Capot de Feuillide was a fervent royalist. A fervent royalist was not a good thing to be in the vicinity of the guillotine! In 1794 he was arrested for attempting to bribe an official of the Republic with the aim of assisting a marquise who had been imprisoned for conspiracy. On February 22, 1794, he was condemned to death and immediately sent to the guillotine.

In her writings Jane Austen loved to satirize popular stories, in which wildly romantic and improbably melodramatic events were presented as the ordinary doings of daily life. Yet, she knew from the personal experience of her close, dear cousin Eliza that sometimes real life was indeed more extravagant—and terrible—than fiction.

6 JANE'S EDUCATION

It has been mentioned that Jane Austen's stay with a foster family was not the only cause of her extended absence from home when she was a child. When Jane was only seven she was sent away to boarding school. The school was run by Mrs. Cawley, the widowed sister of Mrs. Austen's brother-in-law Edward Cooper, who was married to her sister Jane. Jane Austen's sister, Cassandra, was sent there too, along with eleven-year-old Jane Cooper. So, it was quite a family affair in its way, this school business. And, in further explanation for sending Jane and Cassandra there, it has been speculated that the girls' bedroom would have been more efficiently and economically used to put up boys who attended the Austens' school. One more reason given for what (again) seems to us a rather hardhearted treatment of such a young girl is that Jane was deeply attached to Cassandra, and would have been distressed by a long separation from her beloved elder sister. No doubt this is true, but she must have been very homesick even with her sister by her side.

In 1783 Jane went to Mrs. Cawley's school in Oxford, which was soon moved to Southampton. Troops returning to the port city from abroad brought a fever with them that year, and all three girls caught it. They became so ill that they were removed from the school and taken home again. The girls recovered, but so serious was the infection that Mrs. Cooper died from it. (Imagine how close the world came to losing one of its greatest writers before she had written a word of her masterpieces!) The Austen girls spent the next year at home.

After this respite, the sisters were sent off again to a different school. This one was called the Abbey School, run by Sarah Hackitt, who had a cork leg and went by the fancier name of Mrs. (or Madame) La Tournelle—although she did not speak French. One cheerful episode from this time occurred when the girls' brothers, eighteen-year-old Edward Austen and sixteen-year-old Edward Cooper—for cousin Jane Cooper was at this school also—kindly took their little sisters out to dinner at a local inn.

Girls' schools at the time were generally unimpressive at best, and at worst resembled the nightmarish Lowood of Charlotte Brontë's *Jane Eyre*. This second institution was a more wholesome place than the first, but it isn't supposed that Jane learned much in either school—perhaps some dancing, piano, French, spelling, and needlework at Mrs. La Tournelle's— but she did manage to survive to return once more, after a year, to her beloved Steventon home. Jane's formal schooling was at an end.

Girls' schools make several appearances in the novels, and Austen never has much good to say about them as institutions of learning, although she shows sympathy for the women who work in them. Mrs. Goddard, who runs the boarding school Harriet Smith attends in *Emma*, treats her boarders with great kindness, but she cannot be doing much for their minds. A much harsher reference to such places appears in the fragment of a novel Austen began that we know as *The Watsons*. Emma Watson protests that she "would rather be a teacher at a school (and I can think of nothing worse) than marry a man I did not like." Her sister Elizabeth replies, "I would rather do anything than be a teacher at a school. . . . *I* have been at school, Emma, and know what a life they lead you; *you* never have." This exchange also certainly shows that many women were faced with nothing but bad options when it came to figuring out how to provide for themselves in life.

Elizabeth Bennet tells Lady Catherine that she and her sisters "were always encouraged to read." So was Jane, who resembles her heroine in having made good use of her father's library. "Home schooling" seems to have done the trick for the world's greatest novelist. Jane loved to dance and play the piano, and was good with a needle. Proficiency in needlework was an important skill for every woman in those days. However, young Jane's reading by far made up the most significant part of her education.

7 BOYS EVERYWHERE: HOW DID THIS SINGLE WOMAN WRITE SO PERCEPTIVELY ABOUT MEN?

With five brothers at home and just one sister, Jane was growing up in quite a masculine household. Moreover, her parents ran a school for boys in their home. Is it any wonder Jane Austen was able to depict the behavior of men with such accuracy, and their feelings with such sympathy?

We see how much the dispositions and preferred pastimes of spirited boys must have appealed to the young Jane in the characters of some of her heroines. Catherine Morland, the heroine of *Northanger Abbey*, is in fact what we would call a tomboy: "She was fond of all boys' plays, and greatly preferred cricket not merely to dolls, but to the more heroic enjoyments of infancy. . . . she was moreover noisy and wild, hated confinement and cleanliness, and loved nothing so well in the world as rolling down the green slope at the back of the house." As many have pointed out, there is just such a slope at the back of the Steventon rectory. Although Catherine will soon develop a passion for books, at fourteen she prefers "cricket, base ball, riding on horseback, and running about the country" to reading. (Notice that Catherine is playing "base ball" long before its reputed invention in America in the nineteenth century!) In *Pride and Prejudice*, Elizabeth Bennet also shows some tomboyish inclinations when she tramps three miles through the mud to Netherfield Park to visit her sick sister. Rather than moving slowly with ladylike calm, she and Catherine both run excitedly at times, with boyish energy.

Austen also shows an especially perceptive understanding of men's behavior. Just as they are today, women in Austen's day were suspicious of men's motives when their actions resulted in ladies having their feelings hurt or their pride wounded or, indeed, their hearts broken. Women were—as they are today—quick to blame the intentional cruelty of their seducers. Elizabeth Bennet is angry that Mr. Bingley seems to have led her sister Jane to believe he had a serious interest in her only to disappear from the neighborhood as if he had never shown a decided preference for her—and in public! Jane Bennet's more generous impulse is to give men the benefit of the doubt, as we see in this exchange between the sisters:

> *"We must not be so ready to fancy ourselves intentionally injured. We must not expect a lively young man to be always so guarded and circumspect. It is very often nothing but our own vanity that deceives us. Women fancy admiration means more than it does."*
>
> *"And men take care that they should."*
>
> *"If it is designedly done, they cannot be justified; but I have no idea of there being so much design in the world as some persons imagine."*

Jane's position is admirably free of bitter resentment and personal bias and, indeed, later Elizabeth herself will see Mr. Bingley's behavior in this matter "cleared of all blame" by Mr. Darcy's letter.

In *Persuasion*, Anne Elliot goes beyond Jane Bennet's reasonable yet modest defense of Bingley and all men: During her conversation with Captain Harville in which the two are comparing the constancy of men and women in love, Anne says, "I should deserve utter contempt if I dared to suppose that true attachment and constancy were known only by woman. No, I believe you capable of every thing great and good in your married lives." Again and again Austen shows her own belief in the greatness and goodness of men, as well as her understanding of their feelings and motives. She does not excuse bad behavior where it truly exists but shows how labels are incorrectly affixed to men's motives, both good and bad. Women are so very often deceived by their own vanity in their judgments of these very different creatures.

8 PUTTING ON PLAYS

Lacking most of the forms of amusement with which we entertain ourselves today, the lively, imaginative Austen children added something more ambitious to the usual books, musical performances, and card games that might have entertained their contemporaries during an evening at home: amateur theatricals. James, the eldest son and a serious writer, composed the prologues and epilogues for their performances of plays ranging from fine comedy to melodramatic tragedy. Richard Sheridan's *The Rivals* and Henry Fielding's *Tom Thumb* are examples of the former, Thomas Francklin's *Matilda* of the latter. One Christmas they even turned the barn into a real theater—meaning one with painted scenery—and continued to put on new plays even after the holiday.

Eventually James would turn his attention to writing of a different sort, and after 1788 there does not seem to have been any more theatrical activity at Steventon. But surely Jane had been greatly entertained by her older brothers' and cousins' performances (both Eliza and Jane Cooper had participated), and perhaps she had even played small roles herself. Her early writing shows a taste for drama and, not surprisingly, a wonderfully wicked aptitude for parodying the "melodramatic" style of so many offerings in the genre. The dialogue in the novels this young girl would go on to write often gives the impression it would be right at home on a stage: The characters' speech tells the story without needing any narrative to assist it. Moreover, the brilliant comic dramatists of the eighteenth century clearly appealed to Jane's sense of humor and influenced her style of wit.

Given Jane's experience with theatricals at Steventon and her obvious pleasure in learning from and playing with the genre, the response of her heroine Fanny Price to the planned performance of *Lovers' Vows* in *Mansfield Park* is especially puzzling to many. Even without knowledge of this biographical detail, most readers today (and for a long time now) have found Fanny's revulsion at the idea of the adult Bertam children and their friends putting on a play at Mansfield extremely and absurdly priggish. Of course, such activity would certainly show a lack of respect for Sir Thomas in his absence, particularly given the possibly dangerous circumstances of his travels. In addition, the situations and language of the female parts to be taken by the young Bertram women are rather risqué. Fanny is also justified in believing that Sir Thomas would find objectionable the transformation of his billiard room into a theater and his children into thespians, particularly given the involvement of outsiders like the Crawfords and Mr. Yates in the proceedings. (Indeed, when he returns to discover the scheme he extirpates all traces of it, right down to burning every unbound copy of the play in the house.) Furthermore, most people would no doubt sympathize with Fanny's terrified objection to acting herself, given that fear of public speaking ranks right up there with death when people are asked about their greatest fears. But when Fanny so clearly appreciates Henry Crawford's abundant acting talent, and has actually acknowledged that she would be gratified to see a performance if it were not for these other considerations, it is hard for most readers to understand her position. The question of why Austen should give her heroine this role of killjoy in the context of home theatricals when Austen's own family took such great delight in them is a source of endless wonder and debate among critics and "lay" readers alike.

9 BROTHER EDWARD'S FAIRY-TALE GOOD FORTUNE

In May of 1779 the third Austen boy, Edward, was twelve years old. Thomas Knight, a distant Austen cousin (and the landlord of Steventon) visited the parsonage with his new wife, Catherine. Apparently they became so fond of Edward that they asked permission to take him with them as they continued their "honeymoon" travels. This seems to have been the beginning of their extraordinary attachment to the boy, which culminated in their actually adopting him a few years later. The Knights were very wealthy and since they were also childless, Edward stood to inherit their fortune, including several large estates.

Once again, this may seem to show a cold-heartedness toward their children on the part of the Austens—another chance to give them away as they did when they sent them as infants to foster families in the village—but the truth is that the adoption scheme was a great success in every way. The Knights were not only wealthy, but good. Jane was very fond of Mrs. Knight, who was actually the writer's only patron, giving her some kind of annual allowance. And Edward remained very close to the Austen family throughout his life. We may have Mrs. Knight to thank for Jane Austen's novels on much stronger grounds than her bestowal of the "usual Fee" on Jane, for it was Edward's inheritance that ultimately supplied Jane with the comfort and security of the house in which she wrote and/or revised her novels: Chawton Cottage, one of the world's greatest literary landmarks.

Jane makes use of the idea of the child who is adopted by wealthy relatives and keeps some sort of connection with his birth family in several stories, most notably *Emma* and *Mansfield Park*. In *Emma*, Frank Churchill is the son of Mr. Weston, who marries Emma's governess, "poor Miss Taylor." Frank has been adopted by his aunt and uncle, the wealthy Churchills, and—unlike Edward—does neglect his father with the inadequate defense that he is dependent on his adoptive family and dare not fail to comply with their wishes even when those wishes prevent him from fulfilling the other duty. But Frank is too attractive a character not to be forgiven for this lapse. Like Edward, he is, in Emma's words, "the child of good fortune." And Mrs. Churchill is a comic figure whose offstage death provides some of the novel's many laughs:

> *Every body had a degree of gravity and sorrow; tenderness towards the departed, solicitude for the surviving friends; and, in a reasonable time, curiosity to know where she would be buried. . . . In one point she was fully justified. She had never been admitted before to be seriously ill. The event acquitted her of all the fancifulness, and all the selfishness of imaginary complaints.*

How unlike the response Jane must have had to good Mrs. Knight's death!

In *Mansfield Park*, Fanny Price is also being brought up by wealthy relations, her uncle and aunt Sir Thomas and Lady Bertram. In this case, however, when Austen's heroine is taken away at the age of ten from her vulgar, inept parents and large, undisciplined family in their small, noisy, dirty household (where she has nonetheless known the great love of one brother in particular), she is fearful and despondent—but then, her move from one family to the other occurs abruptly when she is only ten years old and she is not treated by her new family as a cherished daughter. The imprint of this childhood grief seems to stay with Fanny until nearly the end of the novel. This is no picture of cheerful, easygoing, happy Edward Austen! As always, through her artistry, Austen transforms those ideas in her novels that seem to have some parallel in her life into something entirely new.

10 THE OTHER WRITER IN THE AUSTEN FAMILY

As we have seen, James, the eldest son, ten years older than Jane, had established himself as the writer in the family long before Jane could have been taken very seriously as such. He was always a good scholar, attended Oxford, and, like his father, was ordained in the Church of England. In 1789, after the verse prologues and epilogues for the family theatricals were behind him, he began publishing his own weekly magazine, called *The Loiterer*. It was modeled after Samuel Johnson's important and wonderful periodicals, the *Rambler* and the *Idler*. Henry, another brother, contributed to it also. *The Loiterer* was published for fourteen months and distributed in London, Oxford, and other major towns in England. In later life James continued to write poetry for the pleasure of his family, but if he had any greater ambition for his writing beyond that, it was unrealized.

It appears that Jane was sometimes irritated by James throughout her adult life. He was her mother's favorite and the other writer in the family, which may have contributed to this friction (if we want to speculate freely). As a male he also had opportunities his more gifted sister would never have—for example, to attend Oxford and travel abroad. And when the Austens moved to Bath, James would take his father's place as the rector of Steventon, which of course meant he also took over the rectory. Jane's surviving letters from the time show that she was annoyed by her brother's perceived eagerness to get settled there, and by his acquisition of a great deal of the family property—furniture, family pictures, and so forth. But in his deep attachment to Steventon and its environs, where he loved to ride and hunt, he also resembled his little sister.

Sibling rivalry and parental favoritism (often of unworthy children) are recurrent themes of Austen's writing, and with such a large family herself she might have seen a bit of both. In any case, the themes show up in every novel. Elizabeth Bennet's character and behavior are influenced by her being her father's favorite, and the same is true of her wild sister Lydia, the darling of her foolish mother. In *Mansfield Park*, Fanny Price's mother greatly favors her sons. In *Persuasion*, Anne Elliot's father, Sir Walter, dotes upon the least worthy child, Elizabeth, because she is very beautiful and resembles him in character. And the rivalry for husbands among the sisters in *The Watsons* is bare-knuckled.

While it's true that Austen's letters contain caustic remarks about James and his second wife, Mary, there is no doubt that the love between brother and sister was great. To soften this somewhat harsh picture further, we might note that James's children, Anna, James-Edward, and Caroline, along with Edward's daughter Fanny, would be Jane's favorites among her many nieces and nephews, and their fond reminiscences of their aunt are invaluable for our knowledge and understanding of her character and behavior.

PART 2

Brilliant Beginnings

11 WHAT DID JANE AUSTEN REALLY LOOK LIKE?

Well, apparently she did *not* look like the familiar portrait so often reproduced. Where did that image come from? It is an engraving taken from a drawing adapted from the pencil-and-watercolor sketch of Jane done by her sister, Cassandra. So the well-known image is at some remove from the original! To add to our uncertainty about Jane's appearance, apparently family members did not think Cass's effort either flattering (like Emma's portrait of Harriet) or accurate. Jane's niece Anna called it "hideously unlike." And there have been other adaptations of the watercolor, one undoubtedly more inaccurate than the next, whether due to altered features or anachronistic attire. So what *did* she look like?

One wishes Jane were not the only family member (aside from the handicapped brother George) for whom we do not have a verifiably authentic formal portrait or at least silhouette. There's even a daguerreotype—an early type of photograph—of her brother Frank. The portraits we have of the rest of the Austens reveal quite a handsome family. But if Cassandra's representation will not do, we can turn to verbal accounts to try to sketch an image of Jane Austen. James-Edward Austen-Leigh, a favorite nephew, described his aunt this way in his memoir:

> *In person she was very attractive; her figure was rather tall and slender, her step light and firm, and her whole appearance expressive of health and animation. In complexion she was a clear brunette with a rich colour; she had full round cheeks, with mouth and nose small and well formed, bright hazel eyes, and brown hair forming natural curls close round her face. If not so regularly handsome as her sister, yet her countenance had a peculiar charm of its own to the eyes of most beholders.*

James-Edward's sister Caroline echoes this description, adding that her neighbors at Steventon thought Jane very pretty. Well, that would mean Jane's appearance had improved a great deal since the age of twelve if her cousin Phila's description of her at that age—"not at all pretty"—was accurate. And her niece Anna also suggested that Jane was at least not conventionally pretty. But all accounts seem to agree that Jane was rather tall, with high color and eyes that sparkled when she was in good spirits. She was probably on the thin side, with curly brown hair and hazel eyes.

Several years ago The Jane Austen Centre in Bath commissioned Melissa Dring, a portrait painter and forensic artist, to create a new likeness of Jane Austen by using the investigative techniques of the FBI. Dring painted a portrait based on written accounts of what Austen looked like, combined with an analysis of the family portraits, and it is startlingly different from the traditional image.

In the end, we can read and weigh the various accounts, and speculate and imagine and reconstruct, but we will never know for sure exactly what Jane Austen looked like.

12 WAS JANE AUSTEN A FASHION VICTIM?

It appears not. Indeed, according, once again, to her nephew James-Edward, "she and her sister were generally thought to have taken to the garb of middle age earlier than their years or their looks required; and . . . though remarkably neat in their dress as in all their ways, they were scarcely sufficiently regardful of the fashionable, or the becoming." There is something sad and spinsterish about this, but it does not, in Jane's case, seem to mark a great departure from her attitude toward clothing even when she was much younger and still might have imagined herself dressing for flirtation and husband-snaring (not that Jane Austen would ever have thought of it in that language!).

Cassandra seems to have been more interested in fashion, and Jane's letters reveal that the younger sister often wrote to the elder about the subject. But if she was not writing simply for the purpose of conveying information (describing dress fabric purchased for Cass's use, for example) then she rarely betrays much pleasure in it. When only twenty-four, Jane wrote to Cass about a ball she would be attending: "I am not to wear my white sattin cap to-night after all; I am to wear a Mamalouc cap instead, which Charles Fowle sent to Mary, & which she lends me.—It is all the fashion now, worn at the Opera, & by Lady Mildmays at Hackwood Balls.—I hate describing such things, & I dare say You will be able to guess what it is like." The last sentence betrays an impatience with "such things" and a refusal to indulge in the traditional female preoccupation with clothes. In another letter about a different ball the following year, Jane wrote, "I wore my Aunt's gown & handkercheif, & my hair was at least tidy, which was all my ambition." Not a very great ambition for anyone with even a little vanity about her looks!

In one letter in which Jane has been describing her efforts to find Cass some embellishments for a hat, she cannot seem to "keep a straight face" when weighing the pros and cons of flowers and fruit: "I cannot help thinking that it is more natural to have flowers grow out of the head than fruit." Since her amused attitude toward fashion resulted in lines like that, we should be very grateful for it.

In a comment on underpinnings, Austen remarks: "I learnt . . . to my high amusement, that the stays now are not made to force the Bosom up at all;—*that* was a very unbecoming, unnatural fashion. I was really glad to hear that they are not to be so much off the shoulders as they were." In another letter, describing young women without partners at yet another ball, Austen again shows her dislike of bare shoulders: "& each of them with two ugly naked shoulders!"

Sometimes people with an unsure grasp of English history refer to Jane Austen as a "Victorian." She actually died twenty years before Victoria ascended the throne, but it is true that her heroines have sometimes been depicted—in book illustrations and on film—as wearing styles actually worn in the Victorian period rather than the Regency. Indeed, Austen herself has sometimes been portrayed in such garb. She might have been happier with the less exposed style of the later period (since she was averse to naked shoulders), but the soft, flowing, classically inspired Regency styles were much kinder to women and much, much more "natural" than the merciless corsets and exaggerated shapes that marked the fashions that followed. It would have been fun to hear what she had to say about *them*!

13 HILARIOUS VIOLENCE AND VICE: THE SURPRISE OF AUSTEN'S EARLIEST WRITINGS

Many people who haven't actually read Jane Austen have an idea of her as a prim and proper writer of ladylike prose, or perhaps a writer of extravagant Regency romances. A reading of her novels, with their sharp, dry wit, splendid nonsense, and intricate exploration of the psychological truths behind human behavior, will completely explode these mistaken notions. But even many of her most passionate fans have no idea how very far from "prim and proper" she can be. Austen's letters are quite revealing in that regard, but the most illuminating evidence of her writerly interest in the vicious, violent, stupid, and silly (more to the taste of raucous boys than refined ladies) can be found in the juvenilia.

Jack & Alice, written when Jane was in her early teens and dedicated to her brother Frank, then away at sea serving in the navy, contains an exuberantly drawn cast of flawed characters: "The Johnsons were a family of Love, & though a little addicted to the Bottle & the Dice, had many good Qualities." After a masquerade, "the Bottle being pretty briskly pushed about by the 3 Johnsons, the whole party (not excepting even Virtue) were carried home, Dead Drunk." Alice in particular pretty relentlessly manifests the family weakness:

> *The perfect form, the beautiful face, & elegant manners of Lucy so won on the affections of Alice, that when they parted, which was not till after Supper, she assured her that except her Father, Brother, Uncles, Aunts, Cousins & other relations, Lady Williams, Charles Adams, & a few dozen more of particular freinds, she loved her better than almost any other person in the world.*
>
> *Such a flattering assurance of her regard would justly have given much pleasure to the object of it, had she not plainly perceived that the amiable Alice had partaken too freely of Lady Williams's claret.*
>
> *Her Ladyship (whose discernment was great) read in the intelligent countenance of Lucy her thoughts on the subject, & as soon as Miss Johnson had taken her leave, thus addressed her.*
>
> *"When you are more intimately acquainted with my Alice, you will not be surprised, Lucy, to see the dear Creature drink a little too much; for such things happen every day. She has many rare and charming qualities, but Sobriety is not one of them. The whole family are indeed a sad drunken set."*

Alice "almost came to Blows" against Lady Williams in one well-lubricated rage. Drunkenness was certainly very common at the time but is very little touched upon in Austen's later work—and certainly not among women! Violence is relished too: The lovely Lucy is caught in a man-trap and then poisoned by a rival who is herself hanged for the offense. And it is all rollicking fun.

14 MORE JUVENILIA

When she was just sixteen Austen wrote a brilliantly funny "unfinished Novel in Letters" called *Lesley Castle*, this time dedicating her work to her brother Henry. Here we can see the beginnings of one of her comic specialties, the monomaniacal talker who thinks of the world as it relates to just one subject and turns all events and all discussions back to the one thing dearest her heart. Mrs. Allen, from *Northanger Abbey*, with her obsession with clothes, is the finest example of this type in the novels. Like *Jack & Alice*, *Lesley Castle* also contains some improper matter for a young girl (never mind a clergyman's daughter) to be writing about—for example, adultery and child abandonment go unpunished.

Miss Charlotte Lutterell is obsessed with cooking. For five weeks she has been preparing the feast for her sister's wedding, but she has just learned from this sister that the groom was thrown from his horse and lies near death:

"Good God!" (said I) "you don't say so? Why what in the name of Heaven will become of all the Victuals? We shall never be able to eat it while it is good. . . ."

"Dear Eloisa" (said I) "there's no occasion for your crying so much about such a trifle. (for I was willing to make light of it in order to comfort her) I beg you would not mind it—You see it does not vex me in the least; though perhaps I may suffer most from it after all; for I shall not only be obliged to eat up all the Victuals I have dressed already, but must if Henry should recover (which is however not very likely) dress as much for you again; or should he die (as I suppose he will) I shall still have to prepare a Dinner for you whenever you marry any one else. So you see that tho' perhaps for the present it may afflict you to think of Henry's sufferings, Yet I dare say he'll die soon, and then his pain will be over and you will be easy, whereas my Trouble will last much longer for work as hard as I may, I am certain that the pantry cannot be cleared in less than a fortnight."

In Austen's later writing we continue to see flashes of this comic exuberance, though her humor is generally more reined-in. But a hallmark of Austen is a wonderful, almost Swiftian combination of neoclassical precision and elegance with talk so nonsensical and/or obsessive it borders on madness. In the juvenilia, violence, drunkenness, and sexual license are thrown into the mix.

Some of Austen's early writing also touches on the themes that will appear in her adult masterpieces. *The Three Sisters*, another "unfinished Novel in Letters," was written in 1792. It explores, as will the later novels, the desperate situations of young women without fortunes forced into a choice between marrying men they do not love, who often disgust them, and refusing these men and possibly getting no more offers—in which case they will very likely descend into poverty along with spinsterhood. But here, as in later novels, Austen is also highly critical of grasping women who, strictly for convenience, marry men they cannot even respect. Austen also contrasts the characters of sisters, as she will continue to do in all her writings. *The Three Sisters* is very funny and often nonsensical, treating the business of marriage with harsh irony. We see a distinctly different approach in *Catharine, or The Bower*, where a marriage of "convenience" is more accurately shown to be what it often was, an act of pitiful desperation, and the matter is debated more seriously and less satirically.

Austen's juvenilia is a treasure trove, giving a fascinating look into the first efforts of this great writer. We can see where she continued, where she diverged, where amplified, where refined. But even if they had no interest beyond themselves, these pieces would be worth reading for their intrinsic value—they are, for the most part, superb.

15 *Love and Freindship*—yes, that's how she spelled it! In 1790, when Jane was just fourteen, she dedicated an ambitious burlesque of a certain type of popular writing, the so-called sentimental novel, to her cousin Eliza. Jane called it a novel, but it is little more than story-length, consisting of a series of letters in which fifty-five-year-old

Laura tells the story of her life to Marianne, the young daughter of a friend, purportedly as an admonitory tale. *Love and Freindship* is absolutely hilarious, and Austen fans who have read only her novels have another great (if quite short) treat awaiting them.

As we have seen, Austen's early writing is very much focused on mocking the contemporary vogue for what she saw as absurdly unrealistic literature. She had an easy target in the sentimental novel, in which extreme emotional responses—both on the part of the characters and, presumably, the readers—were relentlessly manifested. Rational thought is very little in evidence and, indeed, is disdained. Austen also takes spirited delight in writing humorously about violence and the grossly immoral and illegal behavior of the characters. (*Frederic & Elfrida* is yet another hilarious short novel in letters by young Jane that parodies contemporary literature.)

The first convention Austen parodies with Laura is that of the heroine of great sensibility—not to mention beauty, virtue, and accomplishment. In short, she is the kind of female paragon found in sentimental novels, and she has a background that is anything but commonplace: "My father was a native of Ireland and an inhabitant of Wales; my Mother was the natural Daughter of a Scotch Peer by an Italian Opera-girl—I was born in Spain, and received my Education at a Convent in France." A little more exotic than Jane's own upbringing!

In addition to possessing such natural genius that she quickly surpasses all her teachers in mastery of their subjects, Laura has a "sensibility too tremblingly alive to every affliction of my Freinds, my Acquaintance, and particularly to every affliction of my own." When the person knocking at the door is let in to her cottage ("the most beauteous and amiable Youth I had ever beheld"), Laura writes, "My natural Sensibility had already been greatly affected by the sufferings of the unfortunate Stranger and no sooner did I first behold him, than I felt that on him the happiness or Misery of my future Life must depend." In all the writings that follow, Austen rarely departs from this skeptical view of love at first sight.

Austen gleefully explodes other conventions through parody—disguised identity, extraordinary coincidence, the surprise revelation of convenient earlier occurrences, multiple meetings between long-lost family members, and all along the way, histrionics. Not only false behavior but exaggerated, cliché-ridden language is also a target. Thus, characters speak of "the false glare of Fortune and the Deluding Pomp of Title." As one character says, "Where, Edward in the name of wonder . . . did you pick up this unmeaning Gibberish? You have been studying Novels, I suspect."

The exaltation of feeling corresponds to a contemptuous rejection of reason, leading to deliciously perverse speech and behavior. One man scorns to marry the woman he prefers above all others purely on these grounds: "Never shall it be said that I obliged my Father." And when his sister proposes that Edward will have to reconcile with that same father in order to provide his new bride, Laura, with the necessities of food and drink, he responds, "And did you then never feel the pleasing Pangs of Love, Augusta? . . . Does it appear impossible to your vile and corrupted Palate, to exist on Love? Can you not conceive the Luxury of living in every Distress that Poverty can inflict, with the object of your tenderest Affection?" Austen never fails to be amused by willfully unnatural behavior.

And the inevitable—if useless— response of the heroines to distressing situations is to faint repeatedly. Here Laura and Sophia run to the scene of a carriage accident and discover their own husbands "weltering in their blood": "Sophia shrieked and fainted on the Ground—I screamed and instantly ran mad.—We remained thus mutually deprived of our Senses some minutes, and on regaining them were deprived of them again. For an Hour and a Quarter did we continue in this unfortunate Situation— Sophia fainting every moment and I running Mad as often." And if you have never thought Austen sounded at all like Lewis Carroll, you simply have to read the words of Laura's raving to change your mind. Here is a bit of it: "Look at that Grove of Firs—I see a Leg of Mutton—They told me Edward was not Dead; but they deceived me—they took him for a Cucumber."

In her novels, Austen will return to many of the same themes that appear in this prodigious early work, but, alas, there is very little raving of Laura's sort to be found in them.

16 FREINDSHIP? SPELLING AND GRAMMAR

Well, Austen was only fourteen when she made that mistake, but the juvenilia does contain other misspellings. Many good writers are bad spellers, and Austen didn't have the benefit of computer programs to check her work for errors. But spelling was also not completely standardized in the eighteenth century, and people were more accepting of variations. Even proper names were sometimes spelled—or "spelt"—in different ways. In a famous reference to *Pride and Prejudice*, Austen wrote that she had "lop't and crop't" it—where we would insist on "lopped and cropped."

It might be distracting to read whole novels in which common nouns were capitalized in the old-fashioned style Austen frequently used, but some modern editions of Austen's texts bring every instance of her erratic and charming spelling into line with current usage and so we also lose "Swisserland" and "ancle." Somehow Sophia's dying warning to Laura in *Love and Freindship*, "Run mad as often as you chuse; but do not faint" loses something when the spelling of the word "chuse" is updated. (Fanny Price too is amazed to find herself "a chuser of books.") The flavor of a different era is *subtly* retained with such details, whereas many writers of sequels to Austen's novels today, in the mistaken belief that such words are authentically "period" terms, use language that was archaic even in her time!

Because she wrote before the age of certain strict—and rather pedantic—grammatical rules, Jane Austen also makes what many today would deem grammatical errors, using "which" for "that" and "they" as a singular pronoun. (Many today are careful to say "he or she" rather than fall into that agreement "error.") However, we should also note that Austen cared enough about correct language to make use of it in her novels as a way of signaling character.

In *Northanger Abbey*, Henry Tilney jokes about ladies who have "a very frequent ignorance of grammar," and his sister complains that he is always finding fault with her "for some incorrectness of language." He wittily complains about how the word "nice" has completely lost its original precise meaning and "now every commendation on every subject is comprised in that one word." (We might note that his complaint has lost none of its relevance.) Although he is being playful rather than serious and pedantic when he makes these remarks, he clearly does care about the way language is used. Henry Tilney is very closely identified with the author's attitude and opinions throughout the novel, so we can infer that Austen entered into his feelings on this subject too.

One of the things that impresses Emma (to her surprise) about Harriet's would-be lover Robert Martin is the quality of the writing in the letter containing his marriage proposal: "There were not merely no grammatical errors, but as a composition it would not have disgraced a gentleman." Of course, Emma must talk herself out of this approbation in order to keep her predetermined opinion of him as "illiterate and vulgar." Lucy Steele in *Sense and Sensibility* truly *is* vulgar, and her speech is littered with grammatical errors: "It would have gave me such pleasure," "It would have been such a great pity to have went away," and "Anne and me are to go."

Lydia Bennet has grown up in the same household as articulate, eloquent Elizabeth and Jane, whose speech is grammatically correct, but she is quite different from her sisters in a number of ways. It is no coincidence that Lydia, who risks ruining herself and disgracing her entire family by living with a man outside of marriage, also says things like, "Mrs. Forster and me are *such* friends."

Incorrect, imprecise, vulgar language is a clear reflection of character in Jane Austen's writing, but the same cannot necessarily be said regarding speech that is entirely but merely correct, which might indicate nothing more than a good education.

17 LADY SUSAN—AUSTEN'S FABULOUSLY WICKED HEROINE

It does not appear that Jane Austen pursued publication of *Lady Susan*, her completed novel in letters. Rather, we have her nephew, James-Edward Austen-Leigh, to thank for its publication. He included the text, taken from an untitled manuscript transcribed in 1805 (a "fair copy"), in the second edition of his *Memoir of Jane Austen*, published in 1871. It is a fascinating work from Austen's early period, probably written between 1793 and 1795. The consistently high emotion and the melodramatic events and speech in *Lady Susan* also mark it as an early work. There is none of Austen's brilliant re-creation of the ordinary and everyday, which is everywhere in the later novels. It is, however, an astonishingly impressive work for any writer, never mind a girl not yet twenty years old.

Austen's bad mothers in the major novels are mainly guilty of neglect and foolishness, but Lady Susan is downright wicked in her treatment of her daughter Frederica, whom she is determined to marry off very much against her will. This wickedness is also shown in Lady Susan's cool, remorseless indulgence in adultery and her manipulation of others for her own convenience. However, she is also dazzlingly attractive to men and to many women—beautiful, strong-willed, witty, spirited, unsentimental (some of which traits are usefully hidden when necessary under a sweet, gentle exterior). Reginald De Courcy cannot keep the admiration out of his voice when he writes of her, and the two haven't even met yet: "What a woman she must be! I long to see her, and shall certainly accept your kind invitation, that I may form some idea of those bewitching powers which can do so much—engaging at the same time and in the same house the affections of two men who were neither of them at liberty to bestow them—and all this, without the charm of youth." None of the other characters in the story—least of all her good but insipid daughter—can compare to her for attractiveness in the reader's mind either. All the life in the book comes from Lady Susan.

Lady Susan is, as many readers have noted, a kind of immoral version of Austen's witty, spirited heroines Elizabeth Bennet and Emma Woodhouse—and perhaps, even more, of the endlessly debated figure of Mary Crawford from *Mansfield Park*. Just as she does in the case of the winning Miss Crawford, however, Austen makes her disapproval of Lady Susan clear when she has that character say, "I take town in my way to that insupportable spot, a country village." Austen loved the country, and those characters in her novels who do not like it and prefer the "town"—London—must and do have the wrong values. Austen, the clergyman's daughter, cannot condone Lady Susan's smooth deceitfulness and immorality. In spite of this condemnation, though, she draws such a lively, compelling picture of Lady Susan that many think Austen is of Lady Susan's party without knowing it.

In a letter written to Cassandra from Bath in 1801, Jane wrote, "I am proud to say that I have a very good eye at an Adultress. . . . Mrs. Badcock

& two young Women were of the same party, except when Mrs. Badcock thought herself obliged to leave them, to run round the room after her drunken Husband.—His avoidance, & her pursuit, with the probable intoxication of both, was an amusing scene." Austen's letters reveal her wonderfully cool and amused observation of scandalous behavior, and many readers have wished Austen had turned that "very good eye" toward such subjects again in her mature writing. Her voice here reminds us that she is the also inventor of Mary Crawford's daring, worldly remarks in *Mansfield Park*.

Why did the teenaged Austen create such a figure as Lady Susan, a beautiful, clever, spirited, scheming, deceitful, middle-aged adulteress—make her very attractive—and then not seek to have her story published? Why did she never again write a story with such a main character? These are questions as tantalizing as Lady Susan herself.

18 GOTHIC PLEASURES

Although drafts of the novels that would become *Pride and Prejudice* and *Sense and Sensibility* were written earlier, Austen does not seem to have revised *Northanger Abbey* much after 1803—whereas she did revise the others after moving to Chawton—and so *Northanger Abbey* is generally considered her earliest novel. A first draft was written between 1798 and 1799, and some have argued that it was in fact begun four or five years earlier. But we do not have to look to extrinsic evidence to suspect that this high-spirited tale was a youthful work: The style seems to link it both to an earlier period of English history and an earlier period in Austen's development. It is closer in some ways to the juvenilia than it is to the mature novels. Finally, Austen herself asserts that it was the work of an earlier time.

Like so much of her juvenilia, *Northanger Abbey* satirizes contemporary taste in literature, in particular the rage for Gothic novels. It is, in a way, a novel about books. Throughout it Austen is participating in a kind of debate about literature, as she did in *Love and Freindship* and other early stories. Its self-conscious "literariness" is reinforced by the frequent authorial intrusions in which the narrator discusses her "heroine" in the context of what heroines usually are and usually do: "I bring back my heroine to her home in solitude and disgrace. . . . A heroine in a hack post-chaise [the undignified way Catherine must travel home from the Abbey], is such a blow upon sentiment, as no attempt at grandeur or pathos can withstand." It is actually the false Isabella who imitates with precision the heroines of the novels Austen found so preposterously unreal. She proclaims to Catherine (whose brother's fortune will be very modest), "Had I the command of millions, were I mistress of the whole world, your brother would be my only choice" and, we are told, "This charming sentiment, recommended as much by sense as novelty, gave Catherine a most pleasing remembrance of all the heroines of her acquaintance." But there is not an ounce of sincerity in Isabella's pronouncement of this "grand idea," and the heroine ideal perpetuated by Gothic novels is equally—and laughably—false in Austen's view.

As we can see, Austen also discusses what she as the author of a novel is doing—how she departs from convention, how she adheres to it. In the last chapter she writes, "The anxiety, which in this state of their attachment must be the portion of Henry and Catherine, and of all who loved either, as to its final event, can hardly extend, I fear, to the bosom of my readers, who will see in the tell-tale compression of the pages before them, that we are all hastening together to perfect felicity." She does not let you forget for long that this is a fiction she is creating and that Catherine Morland is a character in a novel.

The type of heroine in particular that Catherine is being compared to is the heroine of a Gothic novel. The stock heroine of a Gothic novel was similar to Laura of *Love and Freindship*—beautiful, accomplished, virtuous, and trembling with sensibility. The Gothic novels of the 1790s, the decade in which the Gothic craze was strongest, featured this figure, recognizable as the same type of heroine as that of a sentimental novel, along with other elements we still know today as part of "horror" entertainment: the supernatural; romantic and strange foreign settings; and, of course, terror-inducing plot developments in which the beautiful heroine is threatened with death and worse. *The Mysteries of Udolpho*, by Ann Radcliffe, published in 1794, was the most popular Gothic novel and was greatly imitated. Austen lifts some of this novel almost verbatim in Henry Tilney's teasing description to Catherine of the terrors to be found at Northanger. She is, as is only proper, frightened and fascinated, to his great amusement.

Catherine is young, naive, and not very well educated, but Henry Tilney is older and much wiser, with a mind and voice that seem to reflect the author's. So while Catherine's love of Gothic novels might be dismissed as a sign of her youth and ignorance, we must reconsider when we learn what Henry has to say about the subject: "The person, be it gentleman or lady, who has not pleasure in a good novel, must be intolerably stupid. I have read all Mrs. Radcliffe's works, and most of them with great pleasure. *The Mysteries of Udolpho*, when I had once begun it, I could not lay down again;—I remember finishing it in two days—my hair standing on end the whole time." So it does not appear that Austen denies that Gothic novels can be fun to read. On the contrary, Henry's defense of at least Mrs. Radcliffe's oeuvre is strong, and you suspect that Austen must have relished the thrills as he did. It is rather Catherine's mistake in confusing the characters—called "unnatural and overdrawn" by sensible Mr. Allen—and outlandish plots of Gothic novels with the people and behavior to be expected in the real world that Austen mocks so spectacularly well. That distinction, between fiction and life, is one that her heroines must learn.

19 YOUNG JANE IN LOVE—WHO WAS TOM LEFROY?

Tom Lefroy was the nephew of Jane's good friend Mrs. (or Madam) Lefroy and her husband, the Reverend George Lefroy, of nearby Ashe. He was Irish and the same age as Jane, twenty. She met him when he was visiting his aunt and uncle in Hampshire before beginning law studies in London. He had taken his degree at Trinity College in Dublin, where fellow members of the College Historical Society included Wolfe Tone and

Robert Emmet, who would go on to make history as Irish nationalists and patriots. He had won three gold debating medals, so it seems he was cut out for the law and for Parliament, where he would one day sit.

Tom Lefroy makes a fascinating appearance in the earliest letter we have of Jane Austen's, written at Steventon on January 9, 1796, to her sister, Cassandra, who was staying with the parents of her fiancé, Tom Fowle. It is a lighthearted, gossipy letter in which Jane wishes Cass a happy birthday and tells her the details of the previous night's ball—who danced with whom, who looked good—or not. The excerpt below starts with the second sentence of the letter—that is how soon Tom makes his appearance:

> *Mr. Tom Lefroy's birthday was yesterday, so that you are very near of an age. . . . You scold me so much in the nice long letter which I have this moment received from you, that I am almost afraid to tell you how my Irish friend and I behaved. Imagine to yourself everything most profligate and shocking in the way of dancing and sitting down together. I can expose myself, however, only once more, because he leaves the country soon after next Friday, on which day we are to have a dance at Ashe after all. He is a very gentlemanlike, good-looking, pleasant young man, I assure you. But as to our having ever met, except at the three last balls, I cannot say much; for he is so excessively laughed at about me at Ashe, that he is ashamed of coming to Steventon, and ran away when we called on Mrs. Lefroy a few days ago.*

Jane is obviously enjoying teasing Cass about her open flirtation with the young man, just as she enjoyed "shocking" the assembly at the ball. She shows a self-assuredness about Tom's interest in her—he is "excessively laughed at" because, like her, he is wearing his heart on his sleeve. In this moment she glories in such open display of feeling, but that is something her heroines will be—or will have to learn to be—much more cautious about. Austen seems to say later that it is wrong to make oneself so vulnerable.

In the course of the letter, Tom actually shows up at the Steventon rectory with his cousin George, and Jane must leave off writing. She returns to him again: "He has but *one* fault, which time will, I trust, entirely remove—it is that his morning coat is a great deal too light. He is a very great admirer of Tom Jones, and therefore wears the same coloured clothes, I imagine, which *he* did when he was wounded." Jane certainly seems to enjoy keeping the subject on him!

In the next letter to Cassandra, written the following week, Jane returns to Tom Lefroy and the upcoming ball: "I look forward with great impatience to it, as I rather expect to receive an offer from my friend in the course of the evening. I shall refuse him, however, unless he promises to give away his white Coat." A joke, of course, but perhaps some hopefulness too. And later in the letter Jane promises to give to Mary Lloyd (who will one day be her sister-in-law) all her admirers "as I mean to confine myself in future to Mr. Tom Lefroy, for whom I donot care sixpence." We know how likely it is that she doesn't care for Tom! She goes on to describe how another young man who had been at the ball, John Warren—a friend of Henry's who had attended the Austens' school as a boy and knew the family well—had presented her with a portrait of Tom. This is more evidence that the flirtation was quite a public affair.

However, Jane evidently leaves off and continues writing the same letter on the following day. All has changed: "At length the Day is come on which I am to flirt my last with Tom Lefroy, & when you receive this it will be over—My tears flow as I write, at the melancholy idea." Jane conveys the message, again, in her joking style (rather Elizabeth Bennet–like in its mockery of sentimentality), but it is hard to believe she is really taking it so lightly, that there wasn't something more to their mutual attraction—and some hope on her part that it might lead somewhere. Indeed, when an old man, Tom Lefroy is said to have admitted that he had loved Jane Austen at that time.

So why then didn't anything more lasting come of their very public flirtation? As so often occurs in Austen's novels, it very likely came down to the lack of money on both sides. Jane, of course, had no fortune to bring to a marriage, and Tom had none either. He was the eldest son in a very large family and had five elder sisters. He was completely dependent on the continued goodwill of his great-uncle Benjamin in London, who surely would not have been pleased with such an imprudent match. As things went in those days, he simply couldn't disregard the future of his entire family, who would have been depending on him to marry a woman with money. Perhaps he thought of his own hopes for worldly success as well. In any case, in 1799 Tom married an heiress and eventually lived up to expectations by becoming Lord Chief Justice of Ireland.

Jane never did see Tom again after the day on which she "flirted her last" with him, but almost three years later, in November 1798, evidently with those "retentive feelings" she would give to her heroine Anne Elliot in *Persuasion*, she writes to Cassandra of a visit by Mrs. Lefroy: "Of her nephew she said nothing at all. . . . She did not once mention the name of [Tom] to *me*, and I was too proud to make any enquiries; but on my father's afterwards asking where he was, I learnt that he was gone back to London in his way to Ireland, where he is called to the Bar and means to practise." Mr. Austen here shows a keen and unusual perception of his daughter's longing to know what she is too proud to ask about. And she duly records the answer, an indication of her lingering interest and, perhaps, disappointment.

All of Austen's novels will explore the way money and family interest and influence play all-important roles in promoting and forbidding marriages. The passion with which the issue is addressed might in part, at least, reflect Jane's brief and disappointing romance with Tom Lefroy.

20 CASSANDRA AUSTEN, REAL-LIFE TRAGIC HEROINE

Jane's sister, Cassandra, older by three years, was by all accounts a beauty. So how did she too end up a "spinster"? We just saw that when Jane wrote to Cassandra to wish her a happy twenty-third birthday, the latter was staying in Berkshire with her future in-laws, the Fowles. Tom Fowle and his brothers had been friends of the Austen family since they were students at Mr. and Mrs. Austen's school. They took part in the family theatricals, and at least once Tom delivered an epilogue written by James Austen. By the time of Cass's twenty-third birthday, she and Tom had been engaged for several years. They could not yet marry because—once again—there was not enough money between them to support a household. (Not for them the defiant words of Edward in *Love and Freindship*, "Does it appear impossible to your vile and corrupted Palate, to exist on Love?")

In 1795 Tom, who was at that time a poor clergyman, laid plans to improve their prospects by agreeing to act as chaplain to the regiment of his cousin, Lord Craven, who promised him a good "living" at a parish in Shropshire as his reward for service once the regiment returned from the West Indies, where they were being sent to fight the French. It was during this time that Cassandra was staying with his parents. He was at Falmouth, meanwhile, waiting to set sail with Lord Craven.

If things had gone according to plan he would have returned from the West Indies in May of 1797. Instead, he died of yellow fever off St. Domingo in February of that year and was buried at sea. The Austens all grieved deeply for the young man. James and Tom had been close friends, and James, the poet, wrote a beautiful elegy for him. And Cassandra? Tom had left her £1000, so she would have a very small amount of her own money in the years to come. While she apparently displayed no outward loss of composure, the depth of her feeling can be seen in the fact that she never considered accepting the attentions of another man. Although her toughness shows she was a true Austen, she did not embrace the custom of remarrying by means of which other bereaved family members—

Eliza and James, for example—sensibly moved on with the business of life after a suitable period of mourning. Though Jane's sister was still young and beautiful, her experience of romantic love was over for life.

So how does Jane Austen treat the subject of "second attachments" in her novels? As she treats so many subjects, in different ways in different places. In *Sense and Sensibility*, Marianne, whose opinions are "all romantic," does not approve of them. But Elinor is given the correct—and contrary—opinion in the novel: "And after all, Marianne, after all that is bewitching in the idea of a single and constant attachment, and all that can be said of one's happiness depending entirely on any particular person, it is not meant—it is not fit—it is not possible that it should be so." Indeed, by novel's end, we are told that Marianne "was born to discover the falsehood of her own opinions, and to counteract, by her conduct, her most favourite maxims." That is, she gets over the heartbreak of her first love—for Willoughby—and marries Colonel Brandon, "instead of remaining even for ever with her mother, and finding her only pleasures in retirement and study. . . ." The notion that a young girl would pine forever for a lost love is mocked as a foolish romantic falsehood.

In *Persuasion*, however, sensible Anne Elliot and her former fiancé, Captain Wentworth, both hold on to their first loves—each other—even after a separation of more than seven years, and those the long years of youth. Captain Benwick, on the other hand, is mourning the loss through death of his fiancée, Fanny Harville, when Anne meets him, and she predicts that despite his sorrow, "He will rally again, and be happy with another." When he rather quickly falls in love with Louisa Musgrove, Anne's suspicions are justified. Yet, in this novel, unlike the earlier one, his resilience exposes him as a bit shallow, and his previous "inconsolableness" as demonstrably false sentimentality.

Perhaps Jane was thinking of Cassandra when she gave Anne these lines in her dialogue with Captain Harville on whether men or women are more constant in love:

> *"I believe you equal to every important exertion, and to every domestic forbearance, so long as—if I may be allowed the expression, so long as you have an object. I mean, while the woman you love lives, and lives for you. All the privilege I claim for my own sex (it is not a very enviable one, you need not covet it) is that of loving longest, when existence or when hope is gone."*

Anne might have loved for years while she *thought* there was no hope, but Austen blesses her with a miraculously happy ending—something she could not do for her sister. We may suppose it possible to find as much happiness in writing the world's greatest novels as in marrying and bearing children, but Cassandra did not have that alternative source of joy. In keeping faith—hopelessly—with her dead lover Tom, she became, unlike Austen's creations, the heroine of a tragedy.

21 First Impressions: Why didn't Pride and Prejudice keep its first title?

Jane Austen began writing a novel she called *First Impressions* in October 1796, when she was "not one and twenty," as Elizabeth Bennet puts it. It was completed in August of the following year. By this time it was customary for Jane to entertain her family with her writing, and we can only imagine how she must have delighted them with this effort!

Mr. Austen, good, supportive father—and excellent reader—that he was, thought enough of Jane's story to seek to have it published. On November 1, 1797—losing no time—he sent it to the publisher Thomas Cadell in London with a highly respectful letter asking if Cadell would consider publishing it. Mr. Austen didn't reveal the author's name, but simply compared the length of the manuscript to that of Fanny Burney's 1778 novel in letters, *Evelina*. He even offered to risk his own money to see his daughter's work published.

Well, Mr. Austen could not have received a faster, curter, or—as history has shown—dumber reply: "Declined by return of post."

Luckily for the world, that was not the end of *First Impressions*: Apparently it was read and reread by family and some close friends over the next few years. Two letters of Jane's to Cassandra from 1799 reveal that this was the case. She writes playfully to her sister in January: "I do not wonder at your wanting to read *first impressions* again, so seldom as you have gone through it, & that so long ago." Later that year she writes in the same tone, referring to their good friend Martha Lloyd: "I would not let Martha read First Impressions again upon any account. . . . She is very cunning, but

I see through her design;—she means to publish it from Memory, & one more perusal must enable her to do it." We hear the joyful voice of a writer who knows she is good, and knows that her readers know it.

But it would still be many years before anyone outside Austen's inner circle would read *First Impressions*: it would not be published until 1813, after it had been "lop't and crop't" by its author. In the meantime, in 1800, a novel also called *First Impressions*, written by Margaret Holford, had been published, which probably prompted Austen to change the title of her book.

It is interesting to ask, along with Juliet, "What's in a name?" Would *Pride and Prejudice*—a book with that most famous of titles—be any different if we knew it instead as *First Impressions*?

22 ELIZA: COUSIN AND FRIEND BECOMES SISTER

We've seen that the first marriage of Eliza de Feuillide (née Hancock), ended dramatically with her husband's execution by guillotine. That marriage was marked by another tragedy: The only child of the couple, like Jane Austen's brother George and her uncle Thomas, suffered from an affliction that affected his development. Hastings de Feuillide was physically and mentally weak, suffered from seizures, and would die at the age of fifteen. Unlike the Austens and Leighs, however, Eliza chose to keep her son with her instead of sending him away to be cared for. He had been named after her wealthy and influential godfather—and possibly natural father—Warren Hastings.

Eliza had been a favorite with the Austen family since Jane was a little girl. The two met for the first time when the elder cousin visited the Steventon parsonage after many years spent living abroad. Although Jane was eleven and Eliza twenty-five, the cousins became close friends and remained so until Eliza's death. But Jane was not the only member of the Austen family to show a marked interest in this beautiful, exotic, affectionate, and charming creature: Henry seems to have charmed his cousin in turn, though she was ten years older and a wife and mother. James too was drawn to Eliza. But until her husband met his grim fate, it could only have been playful flirtation all around.

In 1795, when Henry was twenty-four, the flirtation between cousins became something more: He proposed to the widowed Eliza. For some reason, she turned him down. The following year his brother James, now a widower with a young child, also proposed to Eliza and was rejected in turn. He soon found another prospect, Mary Lloyd, who reportedly held a grudge against Eliza for having captured James's heart first—and made sure that she was never, ever, invited to their house. A year after that Henry tried his luck again, and on December 31, 1797, he and Eliza were married. That is a dance worthy of one of Jane's novels!

From their house in London, Henry and Eliza both would do much to see that Jane's novels were published. Obviously, some members of the Austen family appreciated and adored Eliza. Still, others tempered their praise of Eliza Austen somewhat, as James-Edward's remark in the *Memoir* shows: "A clever woman, and highly accomplished, after the French rather than the English mode . . ." he writes. Historically, the adjective "French" has not exactly been complimentary in England, so one wonders about this remark—by Mary (Lloyd) Austen's son, it should perhaps be noted.

Eliza was very musical, and perhaps Jane's own love of the piano was influenced by her. Eliza also played the harp, and maybe Jane was thinking of Eliza's playing when she wrote of that instrument in *Mansfield Park*: "A young woman, pretty, lively, with a harp as elegant as herself; and both placed near a window, cut down to the ground, and opening on a little lawn, surrounded by shrubs in the rich foliage of summer, was enough to catch any man's heart." Eliza, good at catching hearts with or without a harp, died at the age of fifty after a severe illness, possibly cancer. Her death must have been a great loss to Jane—her cousin, sister, and friend.

23 How was *Elinor and Marianne* drastically different from *Sense and Sensibility*?

As Cassandra Austen recalled it, Jane read to the family before 1796 from a novel she was writing called *Elinor and Marianne*. This would have been just after she had finished *Lady Susan*. Like that story, this one was told through an exchange of letters. In 1797, just after she completed *First Impressions* and around the time Mr. Austen was attempting to get that early version of *Pride and Prejudice* published, Jane returned to the manuscript of *Elinor and Marianne* and made some major changes.

Austen not only changed the title of the novel to *Sense and Sensibility*; more important, she changed the way in which the story was told from epistolary—letter form—to direct third-person narrative. We do not know exactly how much revision this change entailed, since we have no manuscripts of any of the versions, but we can pretty safely guess that such a drastic change must have required substantial revision. Why did Austen write novels in letters to begin with, and why did she discard the form in her mature writing?

The epistolary novel was popular in the eighteenth century. Samuel Richardson, one of Austen's favorites, was the major practitioner of the form; Fanny Burney, another favorite writer, used it also. There is speculation that *First Impressions*, the original version of *Pride and Prejudice*, also began as a novel in letters, but we have no clear evidence of that. We do see Austen make very successful use of letters in the juvenilia, but those are mainly short satirical pieces very far from the realism of her adult writing, and she seems ultimately to have found the epistolary form inadequate for her novels. Richardson's *Clarissa* is a very long book, and the artificiality of the letter form in which it is written, especially given the extreme and dire conditions under which the heroine is writing, makes the novel, for all its greatness, something of a joke among many readers who just can't get past the absurdities created by all those unlikely—to put it kindly—letters. (Remember, there were no ballpoint pens or corner mailboxes—expensive paper, tricky quill pens, and bottles of ink were necessary just to begin with.)

The letter form might have suited Austen's juvenilia perfectly because the author herself was generally—and brilliantly—mocking literary absurdities in those early writings anyway. Even at the end of *Lady Susan*, Austen makes a joke at the expense of the very style she has been using. An omniscient narrator, wrapping up matters in a "Conclusion" with the supreme authority none of the individual letter-writers can command, begins this way: "This correspondence, by a meeting between some of the parties and a separation between the others, could not, to the great detriment of the Post Office revenue, be continued longer."

But, after all, in an age without telephone or e-mail communication, letters were truly major facets of life—especially among young ladies and young lovers—and it would be natural for them to show up in realistic novels. Even so, a few of the letters that appear in Austen's third-person-narrated novels strain credulity and show the author's manipulation of the story to a far greater extent than is evident elsewhere in the books. They sometimes appear to be prompted by the need to reveal aspects of the plot previously hidden due to the narrative focus on the heroine, so they don't always share in the perfect illusion of "naturalness" found in the rest of the books. They are also sometimes used to show other points of view and fill in narrative gaps. (Think of the very long letter Mr. Darcy hands to Elizabeth Bennet at Rosings Park, which causes her to reconsider every one of her previous perceptions and judgments.)

Frank Churchill's letter to Mrs. Weston at the end of *Emma* is rather absurdly long, but then Frank has a lot of explaining to do—he must reveal what was really going on the whole time he appeared to be something quite different from what he was. Individual episodes that we've witnessed because Emma was present for them are retold from his point of view. So, while third-person narration might seem to offer more objectivity in

101 THINGS YOU DIDN'T KNOW ABOUT JANE AUSTEN

telling a story, single-viewpoint letters actually help show the whole picture, which in this case was hidden from us; the omniscient narrator did not show all viewpoints as the story went along, but rather stayed very much focused on the heroine's perceptions.

Although Jane Austen moved on from the epistolary form, her novels are still full of letters, and by and large they are wonderfully comic, tragic, suspenseful, exciting, romantic, or some combination thereof, so we happily have the best of both worlds. As with *Pride and Prejudice*, many years would elapse between the time this early version of *Sense and Sensibility* was completed and the publication in 1811 of the novel we know, in which the illicit, shocking, and heartbreaking correspondence of Marianne and her faithless lover Willoughby plays such a vital role.

24 JANE COOPER: ANOTHER COUSIN'S IMPROBABLY ROMANTIC—AND TRAGICALLY SHORT—LIFE

Jane Cooper, the daughter of Mrs. Austen's sister Jane, was very close to Jane Austen and her family. As we've seen, the girls went to the school run by Mr. Cooper's sister, and Cassandra, closer to Jane Cooper's age, was often sent to stay with her cousins in Bath. Her little sister missed her terribly when she was gone! (As Mrs. Austen said with regard to Jane's being sent off to school, "If Cassandra's head had been going to be cut off, Jane would have her's cut off too.") Cousin Jane Cooper often came to stay at Steventon also, particularly after the death of her mother. She took part in the lively family theatricals and must have made a striking appearance in them, because she grew up to be a beauty.

After her father died, Jane Cooper lived with the Austens at Steventon, and in December 1792, she was married at the church there. Tom Fowle, who would soon become Cassandra's fiancé, performed the service. Jane's husband was a naval officer, Captain Thomas Williams, whom she'd met just that past July on the Isle of Wight. They had a very brief courtship: Captain Williams proposed within a month of meeting lovely Cousin Jane, who must have been a romantic girl, because she accepted his proposal.

Captain Williams might have been as risky a choice as Captain Wentworth would have been for Anne Elliot in *Persuasion*, but orphaned Jane Cooper had no prudent Lady Russell to dissuade her from accepting him. Just as would have been true in the case of Anne and Captain Wentworth, Jane was right to trust her young man's confidence in his prospects: Captain Williams was soon knighted for his victories in battles against the French, and so Jane Austen's cousin became, in her mid-twenties, Lady Williams. Though Jane teased her cousin by referring to her husband as "his Royal Highness Sir Thomas Williams," he was Charles Austen's commanding officer and therefore an important figure for the Austens in more ways than one.

Then, in 1798, less than six years after her wedding, Lady Williams was in an accident on the Isle of Wight, the scene of her whirlwind romance. She was driving her chaise when a runaway dray horse ran into it. She was thrown from the carriage and killed. And so ended, sadly, the life of Jane Austen's beautiful young cousin, whose future had seemed to promise enviable romance and happiness for years to come.

25 ARRESTED FOR SHOPLIFTING!

Stories of rich women shoplifting are as scandalous and puzzling today as they were in 1799 when Jane Austen's aunt, Jane Leigh-Perrot, the wife of her mother's brother, was arrested for shoplifting. On the afternoon of August 8 she was accused of stealing a card of lace from a Bath millinery shop. Aunt Jane was not only wealthy, but a dignified, childless, married woman in her fifties. The card of white lace in question did somehow make its way into her possession: it was found on her along with the black lace she had just purchased. She denied having stolen it, and insisted the clerk must have given it to her by mistake. She was charged with grand theft, a capital crime. If she had been found guilty, her fate would most likely have been transportation to Australia—to the penal colony at Botany Bay—for fourteen years. That would of course have been an extreme and terrible sentence for such a woman—almost a death sentence in itself.

We have no record of any remarks by Jane Austen relating to this shocking affair. Her general commentary on her Aunt Jane is not very warm. Still, her aunt should have earned Jane's respect for her dignified behavior during this most humiliating of ordeals, as well as her gratitude: Twice Mrs. Austen offered to send Jane and Cassandra to stay with Mrs. Leigh-Perrot—both at the prison-keeper's house, where she lived for seven months while awaiting trial, and at court—and twice their aunt graciously refused the offer. Her devoted husband did stay with her, however, despite the gout for which he took the waters in Bath.

While the prison-keeper's house wasn't exactly prison, it was a place of Dickensian squalor and chaos, according to Mrs. Leigh-Perrot's eloquent account. While she does acknowledge that the Scaddings family did their best to keep their "guests" happy, her description bears some resemblance to the one in *Mansfield Park* of Fanny Price's Portsmouth home: "It was the abode of noise, disorder, and impropriety. Nobody was in their right place, nothing was done as it ought to be." It was certainly not the kind of abode the rich Leigh-Perrots were used to!

Aunt Jane's eloquence extends to the statement she read in her own defense before a packed courtroom (which held two thousand). She mounts an eminently reasonable argument emphasizing her lack of motive. She pleads her wealth, her want of nothing by way of material goods, her reputation, and her love of her husband. Moreover, she points to the fact that she was found across the street from the shop within little more than half an hour from the supposed time of the crime as evidence of a clear conscience. Many distinguished character witnesses also spoke on Aunt Jane's behalf.

But, as everyone knows, shoplifting is very often the most irrational of crimes, neither motivated by need, nor greed, nor deterred by fear for one's good name. And so, while the jury returned a "not guilty" verdict within fifteen minutes after beginning deliberations, there is still doubt today over Jane Leigh-Perrot's innocence in this affair. The Austens attributed the accusation to a blackmail plot, and many today believe such a plot lay behind the whole business. However, during the trial the defense rather depended on the theory that the white lace was accidentally given to Mrs. Leigh-Perrot along with her purchase. Quite a few people today dispute the notion that Jane's aunt was set up that day in Bath, and believe the evidence rather points to her guilt.

In the same city but in the next century and upon another topic, Jane Austen will have Captain Harville ask Anne Elliot, "But how shall we prove anything?" Anne's reply will have to do for us on the question of Aunt Jane's guilt or innocence: "We never shall."

PART 3

Silence and Disappointed Love

26 WHAT DISTRESSING NEWS MADE JANE FAINT?

"Well, girls, it is all settled. We have decided to leave Steventon . . . and go to Bath." According to family tradition, in December 1800, upon returning to Steventon rectory from a visit to Ibthorpe, where she had been staying with Martha Lloyd, Jane Austen was greeted with these words from her mother, in response to which she fainted. Nigel Nicolson, defender of Bath, points out that James-Edward Austen-Leigh and his sister Caroline both confirm their Aunt Jane's distress at hearing this news without mentioning anything about her actually fainting. Still, that was her sister-in-law Mary's account, as reported by Mary's stepdaughter Anna. It is hard to imagine a young woman as tough and sensible as Jane Austen appears to have been having the same response to bad news that she skewered so hilariously in *Love and Freindship*. To swoon when distressed—that is the penchant of literary heroines of great sensibility like Laura and Sophia, not a twenty-five-year-old Jane Austen!

Mr. and Mrs. Austen had apparently decided while alone at the rectory to call an end to the hard work they had engaged in for so many years at Steventon, hand over Mr. Austen's work in the parish to their son James, and move to Bath. They had certainly earned this change of lifestyle from steady labor to the pleasant, sociable, relaxed retirement they envisioned and seemed to find in Bath, the site of their wedding more than thirty-five years earlier. Mrs. Austen's brother and his wife, the Leigh-Perrots, had a house there. Moreover, Bath was considered a healthful place, and a much better one for young ladies in their mid-twenties who might need husbands.

It has already been mentioned that Jane thought James and Mary a little too eager to move into the rectory, and Jane was clearly unhappy at losing not only her beloved home but so many of its familiar possessions—furniture, pictures, books, horses, and everything in between. Whether or not Jane actually fainted upon hearing of this great change in her life, she had no choice but to learn to live with it: The announcement of the move was made to the girls in December, and by the following May, Jane was living in Bath.

27 DID JANE AUSTEN REALLY HATE BATH?

Jane fainted at news of the move to Bath, tradition has it, not only because she loved Steventon—the only home she'd ever known—very much, but also because she hated Bath—and, indeed, cities in general. Critics and biographers have turned to the letters Jane wrote while she was anticipating the move and detected that she was putting on a good front but was in fact very unhappy. Nigel Nicolson, on the other hand, has argued that that was no front—she truly was not terribly upset at the thought of leaving the country, which he believes had lost much of its earlier charm for her.

Jane describes Bath in a letter as "vapour, shadow, smoke & confusion," which does not sound as if she liked the place very much. Her other letters from the first weeks in Bath are also rather depressed-sounding. "I cannot anyhow continue to find people agreable," she writes rather hopelessly to Cassandra. Jane attends social gatherings and gives reports of them that are either complaints about their disagreeableness or sharpedged jokes about those present. There is little evidence that she was finding life in Bath very enjoyable at the beginning of her stay there. And then there is a three-and-a-half-year gap in the letters. Nicolson suggests that during this period Jane was not depressed but rather enjoying all the lively activities Bath—and the seaside resorts to which the family traveled—had to offer, particularly the dancing she loved, but this position certainly goes against the generally held view of Jane's Bath years.

In any case, it is interesting to see how Bath is presented in the novels. In *Northanger Abbey*, Catherine Morland finds it a delightful place, astonishing in the variety of people and activities it offers, especially when compared to the sleepy country village she has come from. As Mrs. Allen inimitably puts it, "it is just the place for young people—and indeed for every body else too." Catherine more sensibly, if naively, exclaims, "Oh! who can ever be tired of Bath?" Henry Tilney's answer to her probably rhetorical question may hold the key to evaluating Bath's general pleasantness or unpleasantness: "Not those who bring such fresh feelings of every sort to it, as you do." In other words, Catherine "was come to be happy," and thus Bath made her so. Did Jane Austen come there to be happy herself?

Henry Tilney is of course much more sophisticated than Catherine and would no doubt be much more critical and discriminating in judging the place, so when he parrots ironically the required customary complaint that Bath is "the most tiresome place in the world," he notes that it comes out of the mouths of those who every year extend their visits for as long as they can and leave only because they cannot afford to stay longer. So it seems that in fact no one truly tires of Bath in *Northanger Abbey*.

There may be more silly, vain, and vulgar people there than good, wise, and modest ones, but the foolishness of the place is still treated with a kind of indulgence that has disappeared by *Persuasion*, in which the view of Bath is much darker in spite of the fact that the good Crofts and other admirable sailors congregate there. Early on we are flatly told the heroine Anne Elliot's opinion of the place: "She disliked Bath, and did not think it agreed with her—and Bath was to be her home." When Anne sees Sir Walter in his rented accommodations there later in the book, she is ashamed that her father "should find so much to be vain of in the littlenesses of a town." She herself dreads her stay in his Bath house as "an imprisonment." These sentiments seem to be reflected in Austen's remarks about Bath in her letters from this period.

Whatever Austen felt for Bath—love, hatred, or indifference—in *Northanger Abbey* and *Persuasion* she creates two brilliant pictures of the town as it is experienced by two very different heroines.

28 THE MARRIAGE PROPOSAL

Jane Austen never married—but she did accept a marriage proposal. In 1802, two weeks before her twenty-seventh birthday, Harris Bigg-Wither proposed to Jane while she was staying at Manydown House near Steventon on a visit to her old neighborhood. Harris, five years younger than Jane, was the brother of her good friends the Bigg sisters, and she had known the whole family since she was a young girl. Although not a dashing storybook hero—he did have a stammer—Harris was tall and respectable, with excellent prospects. Jane accepted the young man's proposal. They were to be married.

The future, for that night at least, took this shape: Harris would inherit a very large, old, and beautiful estate, and Jane would be its mistress. She would not be an old maid, but a wife and mother, settled close to her family in her beloved Hampshire. She could escape forever "the littlenesses of a town" and, much worse, the danger of remaining "a weight upon [her] family" forever. Perhaps there would be no more novels. Would a lady with so many responsibilities and objects of affection have the time or inclination to write?

But as we know, that was not to be her story. Jane's niece Catherine, one of her brother Frank's daughters, has said her aunt accepted Harris in "a momentary fit of self-delusion" and was "much relieved" when, after experiencing a "revulsion of feeling" during the night (according to Mary Austen, who spoke to Jane within twelve hours of these events), the following day she recanted. Jane evidently told Harris that she had made a mistake and could not marry him after all. It seems she simply did not love him.

The marriage of convenience is an important topic in Austen's novels. In *Pride and Prejudice*, Elizabeth Bennet's opinion of her friend Charlotte Lucas never fully recovers after the latter accepts the hand of the "conceited, pompous, narrow-minded, silly" Mr. Collins (whose earlier proposal to Elizabeth herself is a masterpiece of hilariously unpersuasive rhetoric). However, we must weigh Elizabeth's severe judgment against Charlotte's generally accepted view that marriage "was the only honourable provision for well-educated young women of small fortune, and however uncertain of giving happiness, must be their pleasantest preservative from want."

Charlotte is twenty-seven, plain, and in very great danger of being left "on the shelf." As Austen wrote in a letter to her niece Fanny, "Single Women have a dreadful propensity for being poor—which is one very strong argument in favour of Matrimony." And Austen gave these lines to Elizabeth Watson in her unfinished novel, *The Watsons*: "You know, we must marry. . . . my father cannot provide for us, and it is very bad to grow old and be poor and laughed at." Here too Austen allows for a debate on the subject within the novel. Emma Watson says, "To be so bent on marriage—to pursue a man merely for the sake of situation—is a sort of thing that shocks me; I cannot understand it." But Emma has been brought up in privilege by a wealthy aunt, and Austen's sympathy here is rather with the sister who is resigned to her lack of options because she *does* understand what poverty and spinsterhood mean.

Yet Harris Bigg-Wither was far more attractive than Mr. Collins, and Austen herself could not make that bargain. Some of her heroines are also faced with the decision: Elizabeth Bennet rejects not only Mr. Collins but also rich Mr. Darcy—at least the first time he proposes. Fanny Price will not accept Henry Crawford, although everyone else in the book considers him a great catch. Anne Elliot refuses Charles Musgrove, who is a man of good property and good nature. So, while Jane Austen fully understands why a woman without independent means would feel she *must* marry to secure her future even when she isn't in love, and while she can show some sympathy for those who make that sad choice, when it came down to it, neither Austen herself nor any of her heroines would marry a man she didn't love. For Austen—but not her heroines—that meant never marrying at all.

29 MORE PUBLISHING WOES

Jane Austen began working on the novel we know as *Northanger Abbey* in 1798, just after the tragic death of her cousin Jane Williams (née Cooper). Between 1798 and 1799 she produced a first draft of the book she called *Susan* (not to be confused with *Lady Susan*) although, as has been noted, some believe Austen began it even earlier. In one of the few periods of productivity during this silent time in Bath (relatively speaking, that is—compared to her extraordinary output at other times), Austen copied out and revised the novel she still called *Susan*. This time it was her brother Henry who tried to get it published, as her father had tried to get *First Impressions*—the early version of *Pride and Prejudice*—published by Thomas Cadell.

Henry made the attempt in 1803 through one of his business partners, a lawyer named William Seymour. The manuscript was offered to a different London publisher this time, Richard Crosby. It seemed as though Henry's bid to see Jane's work published had succeeded: Crosby bought the manuscript for £10. He actually went as far as to advertise *Susan* as forthcoming in a brochure called "Flowers of Literature," but that was false advertising of the most disappointing kind—to the author: Crosby would sit on the precious, brilliant manuscript for years.

In April of 1809—with *Susan* still unpublished—Jane would write to Crosby offering to supply him with another copy of the manuscript if the one originally purchased by him had been lost. She boldly informs him that if he does not intend to publish her novel—after having agreed in 1803 to the stipulation that it be published quickly—she plans to seek another publisher who will. Despite her bravado, she asks him to reply to her at the Post Office under an assumed name, Mrs. Ashton Dennis (M.A.D.). Crosby acts quickly enough now: He replies three days later saying he is not required to publish the book and that no one else can publish it but that the author is welcome to buy back her work for the same amount he paid for it, £10.

It must have been terribly disappointing and frustrating for her. £10 does not sound like much, does it? But Jane Austen had absolutely no income of her own; she was entirely dependent on the kindness of her family and her patroness, good Mrs. Knight, and in fact £10 was far beyond her resources. It is hard to compare amounts of money over the centuries, but to put it in perspective, Jane's entire spending in 1807 amounted to around £50. Mr. Crosby would not publish it, and he would not return it without being paid that amount, so the world would continue to be deprived of the thoroughly delightful *Susan*—*Northanger Abbey*—for years to come.

30 "A LITTLE SEA-BATHING WOULD SET ME UP FOREVER."

The Austens, as has been mentioned, did not stay put in Bath during this period but traveled from there to various other resort towns, including Sidmouth, Dawlish, Teignmouth, Weymouth, and, most important, Lyme Regis, which Jane loved. At Lyme she enjoyed "sea-bathing," which was conducted rather differently by ladies in 1804. They would first have to enter a "bathing machine," a kind of cabana on wheels, which was then pulled into the sea so they could emerge from it dressed for bathing without anyone having seen them improperly or indiscreetly attired. A lady could descend directly from the machine into the ocean, aided by a "dipper," a female attendant.

Jane Austen seems to have been very fond of sea-bathing, although she did not swim. In September 1804 she wrote to Cassandra from Lyme, telling her that the bathing that day was "so delightful" that she had stayed in too long and tired herself out and would not go in the water the next day as she had planned. Sea-bathing, like dancing, was another exhilarating sensual pleasure allowed to unmarried females like Jane Austen. She loved both activities.

The title quotation is Mrs. Bennet's testimony to the purported health benefits of sea-bathing in *Pride and Prejudice*, but her daughter Lydia's interest in Brighton has far more to do with the regiment encamped there than with any therapeutic exercise the sea might offer. Jane Austen might have enjoyed seaside resorts in a wholesome way herself, but in her novels they often appear as places with a lax moral atmosphere. Elizabeth Bennet tries to persuade her father not to let Lydia go to Brighton because she fears her sister does not have the character to withstand the temptations of such a place, and she is proved right: While in Brighton Lydia elopes with Mr. Wickham, who has no intention of marrying her. It was at another such resort, Ramsgate, that fifteen-year-old Georgiana Darcy had agreed to elope with the very same man not long before, but unlike Lydia, she had been fortunately prevented from doing so. (And in *Sense and Sensibility*, Colonel Brandon's ward Eliza met her seducer in Bath, another resort though not a coastal one.)

Emma Woodhouse has never seen the sea, but it plays a role in the novel of which she is the heroine. There is a priceless comic dialogue concerning the healthfulness of sea air and sea-bathing and whether or not the John Knightleys did well to stay at South End for that purpose. Mr. Woodhouse gives his opinion on the matter: "The sea is very rarely of use to any body. I am sure it almost killed me once."

More significantly, Jane Fairfax and Frank Churchill met at Weymouth, another of the "watering-places" Mr. Knightley dismisses as "the idlest haunts in the kingdom." Sure enough, it is under the influence of a resort town that Jane agrees to enter into a secret engagement with Frank, "acting contrary to all [her] sense of right." At Weymouth, as Emma puts it, "Her affection must have overpowered her judgment."

But all these seductions and illicit arrangements take place "offstage." Whenever Austen actually places her characters at the seaside, the attraction that locale has for her is apparent. She describes Lyme and its environs at length, praising the great beauty of the lovely, romantic landscape and seascape both, concluding with, "these places must be visited, and visited again, to make the worth of Lyme understood." Anne Elliot and her party make their way to the beach, "lingering only, as all must linger and gaze on a first return to the sea, who ever deserve to look on it at all." That is a powerful compliment from someone who knew what she was writing about, and we can hear the conviction in it.

In the unfinished final novel, *Sanditon*, Mr. Parker's "spirits rose with the very sight of the sea," and Austen seems to enter into his feelings. Charlotte Heywood looks out the window "to the sea, dancing and sparkling in sunshine and freshness," seeming to reflect the author's own delight in this part of nature. Indeed, Emma Woodhouse, who is rewarded at the end of her novel in every way, is granted the extra bonus of a "tour to the sea-side" for her honeymoon with Mr. Knightley. You get the feeling Jane Austen could not have thought of a grander or more romantic wedding present for her heroine.

31 JANE'S MYSTERIOUS DEVON LOVER

Tom Lefroy was not the only man to touch Jane's heart, nor Harris Bigg-Wither the only one to pursue a future with her, if the story handed down in Austen family tradition is true. Many years after the events occurred, Jane's sister Cassandra would tell their niece Caroline (James's daughter) and other young family members at various times that on one of the Austen family's seaside excursions from Bath, Jane met a young man and at least began falling in love again. This is what Caroline wrote of Cassandra's account to her: "In Devonshire an acquaintance was made with some very charming man—I never heard Aunt Cass. speak of anyone else with such admiration—she had no doubt that a mutual attachment was in progress between him and her sister. They parted—but he made it plain that he should seek them out again—& shortly afterwards he died!"

According to Louisa Lefroy, the daughter of Caroline's half-sister Anna, this young man was a clergyman. All accounts of him originate with Cassandra, and what does seem certain in all of them is that Jane's sister thought him good-looking, pleasing, and in love with Jane, who, apparently, returned his interest. Cassandra Austen surely set the bar very high for any potential suitors of Jane's, yet you feel that she approved of this gentleman.

It is not much to go on, but Cassandra Austen was a serious, sensible woman not given to flights of romantic fancy after the tragedy of her fiancé's death and her ensuing complete renunciation of men—a grand and terrible gesture that makes one wish she had in that one instance been *less* romantic. In any case, we can assume there was a good deal of truth in

Cassandra's story. Louisa is most specific in saying this meeting occurred in Sidmouth in 1801, but though we have no certain name, no precise date, no exact place that would enable us to paint a clearer picture of this episode in Jane's life, there seems little doubt that Jane had a romance with a charming clergyman that, once again, ended in sadness and loss.

32 MADAM LEFROY

We have seen how when Jane was twenty years old she had a brief romance with Tom Lefroy that left an impression upon her that lasted for years. But just who was his aunt, Madam Lefroy? She was a significant figure in Jane Austen's life in her own right. The Reverend George Lefroy, Mrs. Lefroy, and their three small children moved into the rectory at Ashe, a neighboring village to Steventon, when Jane was a little girl. Mrs. Lefroy was known as Madam Lefroy and she was indeed an exotic bird, although the wife of a country clergyman. She was a beautiful, elegant, and intellectual woman who read and wrote poetry. She was very kind and helpful to the poor. She was dramatic, enthusiastic, and passionate. Jane became deeply attached to her while still a young girl, and Madam Lefroy became her close friend and mentor.

One of Madam Lefroy's sons has said that his mother hustled her nephew Tom away when it appeared that he and Jane were becoming entangled. Their "profligate and shocking" public behavior in recklessly displaying their mutual interest at the local dances would have alarmed her, since she knew that they could not and must not marry. She would have been looking out for Jane's heart and Tom's future in quickly stepping in to separate them—for life, as it happened. We notice that Madam Lefroy would not even mention Tom's name in front of her young friend in later years. This may seem cruel, but her sons believed she blamed Tom for creating the problem and so she was no doubt still trying to protect Jane's heart in avoiding the subject.

It seems as if Jane might have recalled some aspects of Madam Lefroy and the experience with Tom in her creation in *Persuasion* of Lady Russell, Anne Elliot's beloved friend, mentor, and substitute for her dead mother, who persuades the nineteen-year-old Anne not to enter into what she views as an imprudent marriage with Captain Frederick Wentworth. The novel shows that Lady Russell, though acting out of love for Anne and using her best judgment, has given bad advice. Did Jane ever feel that her own mentor had been overly prudent?

There is no doubt that the loss of her friendship with Madam Lefroy was one of the many severe losses Jane suffered upon leaving Steventon and moving to Bath. It appears that Madam Lefroy suffered the loss too, particularly since her children had grown up by then. She missed her young friend, with whom she had felt such a deep connection and shared so much. And then, on December 15, 1804, Madam Lefroy was thrown from her horse. She died twelve hours later, at the age of fifty-six—on Jane's twenty-ninth birthday.

Four years later Jane wrote a moving elegy for Madam Lefroy, lamenting not only the cruel death of her dear friend, whom she praises most highly in the poem, but also the bitter additional sorrow that her birthday would always call to mind this great loss.

33 DEATH OF A BELOVED FATHER

The Reverend George Austen was a warm, loving father who did all he could to see not only that his ambitious boys succeeded in their professions, but also that his brilliant daughter found an audience for her writing beyond the lucky and appreciative family members who acted as her sounding board. This is even more impressive when you realize that it was long before the age of women's liberation. Moreover, Reverend Austen might have been excused for thinking that much of Jane's violent, vice-filled juvenilia was not exactly suitable material for a respectable clergyman's daughter to be dealing in. Yet he indulged and encouraged her as a child, buying her notebooks and letting her scribble in the parish register the names of imaginary future suitors. In one of the notebooks he gave her he wrote these sweet words: "Effusions of Fancy by a very Young Lady Consisting of Tales in a Style entirely new." And we've seen how he later wrote to a publisher about *Pride and Prejudice*, even offering to put up his own money to see his daughter's book published.

Mr. Austen was a great reader (as well as a writer of sermons), and read aloud to his children from his vast library. He let them look through his microscope, which no doubt delighted them. He let them put on plays in his barn. Altogether, the parsonage over which Mr. Austen presided must have been a good place for a child to grow up in. Although he must have been kept very busy with the duties of the school, farm, and church, Mr. Austen seems always to have found time for his children to an extent that we might have considered a modern development for fathers. He was not a distant figure, but an involved father who gave his boys sensible, shrewd, and affectionate advice when they were beginning to make their way in the world. To add to these virtues, he was also a devoted brother to Eliza's mother, Philadelphia.

It is nice to know that this good man and his (somewhat pricklier) wife enjoyed their few years of retirement in Bath and the other places to which they traveled during this time, and also that the end for him was mercifully brief. Reverend George Austen died in Bath in January 1805. As Jane described his death in a letter: "Being quite insensible of his own state, he was spared all the pain of separation, & he went off almost in his Sleep." It is interesting to note that for all the deaths Jane Austen had to face in her life, she pretty much stayed away from the subject in her mature writing and only dealt with it in a broadly comical way in the juvenilia, before she had much experience of it.

In addition to having to grieve this terrible loss, a problem of a practical nature now faced Jane, her mother, and her sister: how and where to live. The Church of England did not make any provisions for the widows and children of clergymen, and so the Austen women were completely dependent on the men in the family for the solution to this problem. Mr. Austen's death was a blow indeed.

34 Why was *The Watsons* left unfinished?

The Watsons holds an interesting place in Jane Austen's writing, being the only major piece of writing begun—and ended, though left unfinished—during this largely silent middle period. Many of her biggest fans haven't read it or even heard of it, but it is a wonderful—if frustrating—fragment, quite deserving of a large audience.

As with *Lady Susan*, we have Austen's nephew, James-Edward Austen-Leigh, to thank for the publication of *The Watsons*. He included it also in the second edition of his *Memoir* of his aunt, published in 1871. The paper on which *The Watsons* was written is watermarked 1803. A granddaughter of Jane's brother James, Fanny Lefroy, has said that the novel was begun in Bath in 1804. There has been much speculation about why Austen never finished this promising story. Austen-Leigh himself puts forth a theory:

> *My own idea is, but it is only a guess, that the author became aware of the evil of having placed her heroine too low, in such a position of poverty and obscurity as, though not necessarily connected with vulgarity, has a sad tendency to degenerate into it: and therefore, like a singer who has begun on too low a note, she discontinued the strain. . . . [C]ertainly she never repeated [the error] by placing the heroine of any subsequent work under circumstances likely to be unfavourable to the refinement of a lady.*

This is an interesting theory, but the idea that a distaste for low matters would have cut short Austen's work on this story might rather be a reflection of Austen-Leigh's own sensibility than hers. To illustrate this, we might note that in one of Jane's letters to Cassandra that he includes in the *Memoir*, he excises the part of a sentence where Austen expresses the hope that her little niece hasn't filled her bed with fleas! But consider (again) these lines from *Mansfield Park*, describing the heroine's Portsmouth home:

> *It was the abode of noise, disorder, and impropriety. Nobody was in their right place, nothing was done as it ought to be. . . . [H]er father . . . was more negligent of his family, his habits were worse, and his manners coarser, than she had been prepared for. . . . [H]e swore and he drank, he was dirty and gross. . . . [H]e scarcely ever noticed her, but to make her the object of a coarse joke.*

Nothing in *The Watsons* is "low" enough even to approach that depth. And in *Persuasion*, Anne Elliot is happier to visit Mrs. Smith, a poor invalid whose living quarters are "limited to a noisy parlour, and a dark bed-room behind," than to spend the evening with her rich aristocratic cousins, the Dalrymples. It is clear that Sir Walter's revulsion at his daughter's preference reflects not his true refinement but his contemptible vanity and shallowness: "Upon my word, Miss Anne Elliot, you have the most extraordinary taste! Every thing that revolts other people, low company, paltry rooms, foul air, disgusting associations are inviting to you."

Certainly as a literary subject, as a backdrop for her heroines, Austen did not completely reject unrefined circumstances. In the case of *The Watsons*, a distinction is made between a lack of money and a lack of breeding.

In fact, the significance of "refinement" itself becomes one of the themes of the story as we have it, and one wonders what else Austen would have done with the subject had she continued. So, far from wishing to avoid the issue of vulgarity, Austen focuses upon it.

The Watson family is poor, but clearly there is nothing vulgar in Elizabeth Watson's need to keep busy with the family's "great wash"—the laundry—and the Osbornes, although in possession of title, wealth, and castle, are careless of the feelings of others. Lord Osborne seems incapable of intelligent conversation. Tom Musgrave, a young man with an independent fortune, has a rakish charm but not the perfect manners of a gentleman. When the two pay an unexpected visit to the home of the Watsons just as the family is about to eat a humble, inelegant meal, Emma, "having in her aunt's family been used to many of the elegancies of life, was fully sensible of all that must be open to the ridicule of richer people in her present home." In contrast, "[o]f the pain of such feelings, Elizabeth knew very little;—her simpler mind or juster reason saved her from such mortification. . . ." Austen here stands behind Elizabeth's "honest simplicity" and lack of shame. Why indeed should these sisters be the ones ashamed when Emma herself knows the visit has "quite as much impertinence in its form as good breeding"?

Their brother Robert, a prosperous lawyer, speaks to Emma quite rudely, and his wife, who brought her own fortune to the marriage, is snobbish and phony, with manners that are "pert and conceited." One thing this short piece of writing makes clear is that people with money can be quite ill-bred.

If James-Edward Austen-Leigh's guess about why *The Watsons* was never completed is off the mark, perhaps the reason is another one often suggested: that the death of Mr. Austen in January 1805 effectively ended Jane's work on it. According to Cassandra, Jane had planned to kill off Mr. Watson, who is sickly throughout, in the course of the novel. While the death of a beloved father would in itself have been enough reason for someone in her already unsettled condition to leave off writing, perhaps the story she was working on hit Austen a little too close to home, and in more ways than one. The death of Mr. Watson would leave his unmarried daughters in desperate financial straits, having then to acquire husbands at any cost or accept the precarious and painful fate of being old maids entirely dependent on the kindness of their brothers, a situation also perhaps too familiar to Jane Austen.

Whatever the reason it was left unfinished, we can only enjoy the little we have of a delightful story, and wish that Jane Austen had chosen to complete *The Watsons*.

35 THE OTHER EMMA

It is sometimes suggested that *The Watsons* was an early version of *Emma*—for the obvious reason that the heroines have the same first name. But there is little other resemblance, and in the story of a family of sisters (although this one also includes brothers) who have to find husbands, it is actually closer to *Pride and Prejudice*. Emma Watson's position also somewhat resembles that of Fanny Price and Frank Churchill in *Mansfield Park* and *Emma* respectively; both of those characters were taken in as children and brought up by wealthy aunts and uncles. Jane Austen's own brother Edward was, of course, also adopted by wealthy relatives. In none of these cases was the child an orphan, which is what makes it somewhat strange to our way of thinking.

As *The Watsons* begins, Emma's rich aunt has remarried and the new husband does not want Emma around, so she has been sent back to live with her poor father and siblings. As her brother Robert tactfully phrases it to her, "sent back a weight upon your family, without a sixpence"—for now she, like her sisters, must either find a husband or remain a burden on the family—on himself in particular, no doubt Robert quite rightly fears. Emma comes to them with the "refinement" and self-assurance of an heiress—indeed, of an Emma Woodhouse—but without the fortune of one.

Emma is a most attractive heroine, very pretty, proud, and confident, and in these qualities she resembles Elizabeth Bennet and, again, Emma Woodhouse, but she also possesses a thoughtfulness and selflessness at times more like that of Anne Elliot in *Persuasion*. One of the most charming scenes in all of Austen's writings appears in this fragment, and it beautifully shows Emma Watson's character.

Aristocratic Miss Osborne has been promising all week to dance the first two dances of the first winter ball with a little boy close to her family, ten-year-old Charles Blake. When she breaks her promise and dances them instead with one of the officers, the little boy is devastated:

He stood the picture of disappointment, with crimsoned cheeks, quivering lips, and eyes bent on the floor. . . . though he contrived to utter with an effort of boyish bravery "Oh! I do not mind it,"—it was very evident by the unceasing agitation of his features that he minded it as much as ever.—Emma did not think, or reflect;—she felt and acted—.

"I shall be very happy to dance with you sir, if you like it" said she, holding out her hand with most unaffected good humour.

This kind act of Emma's immediately restores all little Charles's joy, and the spirit with which she performs it, and the lack of vanity and self-consciousness that might have held an inferior character back from such a bold gesture (she is making her first public appearance in this town, after all), make her a very intriguing, if unfinished, picture of a heroine.

36 SOUTHAMPTON

After the death of Mr. Austen, Jane's brothers came together, figuratively speaking, each promising to contribute something annually to the support of their mother and sisters. (Except for George, the handicapped brother, of course, and Charles, who was far away at sea, and could not help.) Mrs. Austen and Cassandra had a little money of their own, but Jane had none. In 1806, the three women left Bath for good, as Jane later wrote feelingly, "with what happy feelings of Escape!"

From October 10 of that year until April 1809 Jane Austen lived in Southampton, where she shared a home with her mother; her sister, Cassandra; her good friend Martha Lloyd (the sister of James Austen's wife Mary); her brother Frank; and his new bride, Mary, who was pregnant when they moved in. They lived for five months in cramped quarters, where Jane's patience was tried, as her grumpy letters from this time attest: She complains to Cassandra after a visit from her brother James, Mary, and baby Caroline of the "torments of rice puddings and apple dumplings." Poor Jane, never able to avoid company or spend her time as she wished! They then all moved to a spacious house with a garden in Castle Square. Jane's spirits seem to have been raised by the garden, in which she took an active interest. Frank became captain of the *St. Albans* and departed, leaving behind him in Southampton a household of five women.

Then the family suffered a terrible shock: In October 1808 Edward Austen's wife, Elizabeth, died a few days after giving birth to her eleventh child. The exact cause of her death is a mystery, but she was only thirty-five years old. Jane immediately expressed an interest in minding two of her nephews, and less than two weeks after their mother's death Edward and George, ages thirteen and fourteen, arrived in Castle Square. Now Jane was called upon to use all the knowledge of boys she had acquired growing up surrounded by brothers and the pupils in the boys' school run by her parents. She distracted her nephews from their grief by playing games with them—cards, ball games, pick-up sticks. They shot at paper boats with horse chestnuts. Jane took them out on the river, letting them row, and she took them to see a seventy-four-gun battleship under construction. Jane came through beautifully for her nephews, showing once again her understanding of and affinity with children, though she had none of her own.

In the fall of 1808 a decision was made in the Austen family that cheered Jane immensely. Her letters throughout the following winter and spring show rising spirits and energy that we can safely attribute to that decision. It is at this point that Jane feels entitled and confident enough to write to Crosby, the publisher, to inquire about *Northanger Abbey,* the novel he had purchased six years earlier. Later, in the summer of 1809, the decision that had been made was put into effect. Jane Austen and her household of women would move once again, changing everything.

PART 4

The Glorious Years

37 EDWARD TO THE RESCUE

Edward Austen, the third son, had been the rich and lucky one until left a widower by the death of his beloved wife Elizabeth. He was still rich, however, and he now offered his mother and sisters, who were living in Southampton, the choice of two houses—one near his estate Godmersham in Kent, the other in Chawton, a village in their native Hampshire. They chose the county they knew and loved best, and so, in 1809, the four women (Martha Lloyd was still part of the household) moved into Chawton Cottage, a comfortable red brick house with six bedrooms and an appealing garden. Another of Edward's estates, Chawton House, was a short walk away. Martha and Mrs. Austen had their own bedrooms and although there were enough bedrooms to go around, Jane and Cassandra chose to share a room with two beds, just as they had done at Steventon.

Jane would rise early, go downstairs, and practice the piano before the others got up. One of her only chores was to make breakfast for everyone. She was also in charge of the sugar, tea, and wine stores. Although they had a maid and a cook, Martha seems to have done much of the cooking. We have her recipe book as evidence of this. Mrs. Austen, though in her seventies, loved to work in both the vegetable and flower gardens.

The house was situated at the junction of three main roads so that coaches flew past the house several times a day, some of them rattling beds and windows. For all its rural sleepiness, Chawton was not so far removed from the world as one might have expected. So short was the distance between coach road and house that passengers and occupants could eye each other. Mrs. Knight, Edward's adoptive mother, received a report from a gentleman riding by in a post-chaise that the family looked "very comfortable at Breakfast." Edward had one of the front windows blocked up and a new window cut into the side for more privacy and a prettier view.

The most significant aspect of this return to rural Hampshire is that it seems to have inspired Jane to return to her writing. Chawton Cottage is one of the great literary shrines of the world because within its humble walls six of our greatest novels were first written or given their final form. This return to creativity began when Jane took out the manuscript of *Sense and Sensibility* she'd been carrying around with her through all her changes of residence over the years since leaving Steventon and started to revise it. Settled once again in the Hampshire countryside, in a permanent home with a comfortable routine, she got back to work.

38 THE CREAKING DOOR

Jane's nephew, James-Edward Austen-Leigh, wrote this now-famous description of his aunt's habits of composition at Chawton:

> *She had no separate study to retire to, and most of the work must have been done in the general sitting-room, subject to all kinds of casual interruptions. She was careful that her occupation should not be suspected by servants, or visitors, or any persons beyond her own family party. She wrote upon small sheets of paper which could easily be put away, or covered with a piece of blotting paper. There was, between the front door and the offices, a swing door which creaked when it was opened; but she objected to having this little inconvenience remedied, because it gave her notice when anyone was coming.*

Austen-Leigh's sister Caroline confirms this picture of their aunt's writing habits in her own, shorter memoir: "My aunt must have spent much time in writing—her desk lived in the drawing room. I often saw her writing letters on it, and I believe she wrote much of her Novels in the same way—sitting with her family, when they were quite alone; but *I* never saw any manuscript of *that* sort, in progress."

Some have expressed the opinion that this cannot be the whole truth of the matter and that Austen could not in particular have revised her novels in that furtive way. This, however, is the story that has been handed down by those who were there, and all else must be mere speculation. It's hard to think that the woman who could have written such novels to begin with could not have revised them while standing on her head if she had wanted to!

39 Today's "self-published" writers are in good company: *Sense and Sensibility*

Jane Austen, settled in her latest and final home in Chawton Cottage, was now revising one of the novels she had begun so many years earlier. (Nigel Nicolson, rejecting the mainstream positive view of this latest relocation, says Austen turned to her manuscripts again after living in the more interesting towns of Bath and Southampton, "having nothing else to do.") She was once again working on *Sense and Sensibility*, originally the novel in letters she called *Elinor and Marianne*.

We've seen how Austen mocked excessive sensibility in the juvenilia, particularly in the hilarious burlesque *Love and Freindship*. Marianne is not possessed of—or afflicted with—sensibility to the absurd extent Laura and Sophia are, but she still has quite a potent degree of it in her character. Still, the title *Sense and Sensibility* sometimes misleads readers into expecting completely antithetical characters in the two sisters, while in fact both Elinor and Marianne can claim sense *and* sensibility. It is not a matter of each girl having one or the other, but rather the proportion of each quality to be found in the two sisters that is under consideration.

The portrait of Marianne does sometimes verge on caricature, for example when she:

> would have thought herself very inexcusable had she been able to sleep at all the first night after parting from Willoughby. She would have been ashamed to look her family in the face the next morning, had she not risen from her bed in more need of repose than when she lay down in it. . . . She spent whole hours at the pianoforté alternately singing and crying; her voice often totally suspended by her tears.

Still, there is no denying the overall appeal of Marianne's ardent manner, her passion for poetry, music, and nature: "In her eyes, which were very dark, there was a life, a spirit, an eagerness which could hardly be seen without delight." Although she must learn—through a physical ordeal brought on by her passion for a faithless lover that brings her very close to death—to subdue her excessively romantic principles and impulses, some readers have always found the severity of her chastisement and her fate at the end of the novel hard to accept. But then our culture is more thoroughly "romanticized" than was the culture of Austen's day, so we probably have a harder time seeing passionate romanticism lose out to Elinor's more rational and altruistic mode of conduct than many readers did then.

Once again, Henry Austen stepped in to help Jane find a publisher. He took his sister's manuscript to Thomas Egerton of the Military Library, Whitehall, who in 1810 agreed to publish it "on commission," meaning at the author's expense, including fees for advertising and distribution. It was "Printed for the Author" in 1811, anonymously, with Henry and Eliza's money. Jane requested that everyone who was in on her authorship keep it a secret.

Jane stayed with Henry and Eliza in London while she corrected the proofs, and while there she wrote these moving, unguarded words to Cassandra: "No indeed, I am never too busy to think of S&S. I can no more forget it, than a mother can forget her sucking child." Throughout the letters, when Austen writes of her novels and her heroines, her voice is often that of a mother speaking tenderly of her children.

40 FIRST SUCCESS

We don't know how many copies of *Sense and Sensibility* were printed—750 or 1,000—but the first edition had sold out by July of 1813. Jane Austen had made a profit of £140 and the few reviews in the press were good. Also good were word-of-mouth reviews: It was discussed at gatherings in high society, and people raved about it in letters to family and friends. Even the royal family was impressed. Fifteen-year-old Princess Charlotte wrote, "I have just finished reading; it certainly is interesting, & you feel quite one of the company. I think Maryanne & me are very like in disposition, that certainly I am not so good, the same imprudence, &c, however remain very like. I must say it interested me much."

Now, after so many years and so many trials, Jane Austen was seeing her first "child" in print and what's more, she was learning that people were buying it, and reading it, and finding it interested them much.

41 "Light & bright & sparkling"

With the success of *Sense and Sensibility*, the publisher was certainly interested in Jane Austen's next novel. In revising *First Impressions*, the novel she had begun in 1796, which her father had unsuccessfully tried to have published, Jane made the manuscript quite a bit shorter than the version Mr. Austen had sent to Thomas Cadell. Thomas Egerton offered £110 for the novel she now called *Pride and Prejudice*, and although Jane had hoped for more, she accepted his offer, apparently to save Henry (and Eliza) from having to advance money again. *Pride and Prejudice* was published in January 1813.

The reviews and general public response to this new novel were even more enthusiastic than they had been for *Sense and Sensibility*. Once again, Austen could enjoy the direct praise of only a few people because this book, too, was published anonymously, "by the Author of *Sense and Sensibility*." In those days, ladies did not seek to draw public attention to themselves. Rather than basking in the limelight of successful authorship, Jane was quietly living in the Hampshire countryside. After the publication of the book Jane so lovingly—and rightly—referred to as "my own darling Child," she and Mrs. Austen took turns reading from it to their neighbor, a poor spinster named Miss Benn. What an extraordinary picture that must have made, and all the more amusing because Miss Benn—also kept in the dark about Jane's secret—did not know she was in the presence of the author!

Letters from this time reveal Jane grumbling to Cassandra about their mother's way of reading the dialogue aloud—Jane thinks she reads too quickly and doesn't quite get the characters' voices right—and gushing to her sister about her own creation, the heroine of *Pride and Prejudice*, Elizabeth Bennet: "I must confess that *I* think her as delightful a creature as ever appeared in print, & how I shall be able to tolerate those who do not like *her* at least, I do not know." Austen complains of a few typographical errors and expresses her belief that a "said he" or "said she" would make things clearer, but on the whole she is obviously delighted, and her exasperation over her mother's reading does not really mar her pleasure. Her mood is one of exultation, and she writes teasingly to Cass:

> *Upon the whole however I am quite vain enough & well satisfied enough. —The work is rather too light & bright & sparkling;—it wants shade;—it wants to be stretched out here & there with a long Chapter—of sense if it could be had, if not of solemn specious nonsense—about something unconnected with the story; an Essay on Writing, a critique on Walter Scott, or the history of Buonaparte—or anything that would form a contrast & bring the reader with increased delight to the playfulness & Epigrammatism of the general stile.*

Too light and bright and sparkling indeed! In the highest of spirits, Austen wrote to her sister with the wit and playfulness of Elizabeth Bennet herself.

42 A TRUTH UNIVERSALLY ACKNOWLEDGED

It is a truth universally acknowledged that the first line of *Pride and Prejudice* is the best and most famous opening sentence in English literature and the gateway to one of the world's greatest pleasures. So it is surprising to see the mild praise of the novel that appears in reviews written at the time it was first published. These reviews were favorable, as they had been in response to *Sense and Sensibility*, but they focused approvingly on the book's morality and barely seemed to notice its breathtaking wit! However, there was a difference in tone between published reviews of *Pride and Prejudice* and social gossip about it, and the latter was much more interesting and spirited.

The first edition of 1,500 copies had sold out by July of 1813. A second edition was published that fall, and a third would be published in 1817. It was *the* novel to read or, as Anne Isabella Milbanke (who would later marry Lord Byron) put it, it was "at present the fashionable novel." Maria Edgeworth, whom Jane admired, read it and urged her brother in a letter to do so also. Warren Hastings praised it, to Jane's delight. The playwright Richard Sheridan said *Pride and Prejudice* "was one of the cleverest things" he had ever read. (We recall that the Austen children put on Sheridan's play *The Rivals* at the Steventon rectory.) The high praise from prominent writers must have been especially gratifying to Austen.

We've seen that *Pride and Prejudice* was published anonymously, which was how Jane liked it. As a result, however, many people had the wrong woman down as the author—and others thought it too good to have been written by a woman at all. Henry Austen, though sworn to secrecy like the rest of those in the know, let slip the secret of Jane's authorship more than once. Jane forgave him since his motivation was rooted in "Brotherly vanity and Love"—and of course because it was Henry—but she appreciated the superior discretion of her brother Frank and his wife.

From poor Miss Benn to the highest members of high society, Elizabeth Bennet was working her charm while her creator watched and listened with amusement and satisfaction.

43 WHICH OF JANE'S HEROINES DID HER MOTHER CALL "INSIPID"?

According to notes left by Cassandra Austen, Jane's next novel, *Mansfield Park*, was begun in February 1811 and finished in the summer of 1813. This was the first of Austen's novels entirely written in this later period rather than being a revision of one first composed in the eighteenth century. Thomas Egerton would publish this novel, as he had *Sense and Sensibility* and *Pride and Prejudice*, but either he knew it was not the crowd-pleaser that *Pride and Prejudice* was and offered to publish it only on commission or he offered an unacceptably low price for the copyright. In either case, this novel was published on commission also. The first edition of probably 1,250 copies was published in May 1814 and sold out within six months, so it was surprising and disappointing when Egerton declined to publish a second edition. His instincts were right: When Henry negotiated with a different publisher to bring out a second edition in 1816—also on commission—it did not sell, and was remaindered the following year. Perhaps Austen's own comment that this novel was "not half so entertaining" as *Pride and Prejudice* expressed the common view.

To Jane's disappointment, there were no contemporary reviews of *Mansfield Park*. (Again, serious authors whose work is ignored by the press today can perhaps take some comfort in that fact.) We do, however, have a fascinating document containing responses to the novel: Jane herself recorded the opinions of *Mansfield Park* expressed by family, friends, neighbors, and other acquaintances. One opinion that does indeed show up repeatedly is that it is not as good as *Pride and Prejudice*. Frank Austen and his wife Mary felt this way; so did Edward and his sons Edward and George; Mrs. Austen; Charles; and Jane's friend, the Godmersham governess, Anne Sharp.

Jane notes that many of the readers do like the heroine, Fanny Price, among them Frank, Edward, and his son Edward and daughter Fanny. Martha and Cassandra both approve of her. But there are strong objections to the heroine also, such as can't be imagined in the case of Elizabeth Bennet or Elinor and Marianne Dashwood. Jane records praise and censure equally without comment. Edward's son George disliked Fanny and preferred Mary Crawford. His brother Edward also flew in the face of the author's intentions in preferring the witty Henry Crawford to the hero Edmund, calling the latter "cold and formal."

Anna, Jane's intelligent, spirited niece, "could not bear Fanny." The strength of her disgust comes through loud and clear! And Mrs. Austen, no slouch in the intelligence department herself, "thought Fanny insipid"—as many readers have thought since. Jane's brother Henry admired Henry Crawford, and Jane seems to feel the need to qualify his opinion: "I mean properly—as a clever, pleasant Man."

It is interesting to see that while many readers—particularly since around the middle of the twentieth century—have in fact found *Mansfield Park* the most interesting, sophisticated, and complex of Austen's novels, and certainly the most difficult to "figure out," the general opinion is no doubt the same that was heard by Jane—*Pride and Prejudice* is preferred. And, as members of her own family did at the time of the book's publication, many readers continue to dislike the heroine Fanny—and the hero Edmund, for that matter—and much prefer the morally corrupt but very entertaining figures of Mary and Henry Crawford.

44 Dedicated to the one I hate: Jane and the Prince Regent

1811, the year Austen started writing *Mansfield Park*, was the year that George, Prince of Wales, was appointed prince regent. His father, King George III, was insane and therefore incompetent to rule, although he remained monarch until his death in 1820. The Prince Regent threw himself an enormously expensive and lavish party to celebrate, which the nation certainly could not afford but which was right in keeping with the general behavior of the decadent, fashionable, and immoral princes. Vice and scandal tainted the royal household, with adultery and gambling just some of the popular activities among its members.

Many readers have seen in *Mansfield Park* Jane Austen's commentary on Regency London. Mary and Henry Crawford arrive in Mansfield from town and bring into its quiet, traditional spaces and pastimes seductive energy, wit, sophistication, and artistic power, but also, "a perversion of mind," "blunted delicacy and"—again—"a corrupted, vitiated mind," and "cold-blooded vanity." London is also the scene of much of the bad behavior of Maria, Julia, and Tom Bertram, the children of the Mansfield household. The superficial glamour and fashionable amusements of Regency London are contrasted with the solid principles and true morality to be found only outside of the city, with its bad royal influences. Those traditional values are upheld by the book's heroine, Fanny Price.

When she was much younger, Jane had enjoyed joking about the evils of the great city. In *Love and Freindship*, Isabel warns Laura, "Beware of the insipid Vanities and idle Dissipations of the Metropolis of England," and in a letter to Cassandra from London Jane writes, "Here I am once more in this Scene of Dissipation & vice, and I begin already to find my Morals corrupted." It seems as if the silly caricature of London that once delighted Jane has now almost become the sordid reality.

Whether or not Austen subtly worked her opinion of the Prince Regent into *Mansfield Park*, she stated it flatly in a letter in response to the public battles of the Regent and his wife, in which the Prince accused the Princess of adultery and she now defended herself in a letter to the *Morning Chronicle*. Jane wrote: "I suppose all the World is sitting in Judgement upon the Princess of Wales's letter. Poor Woman, I shall support her as long as I can, because she *is* a Woman, & because I hate her Husband."

So how, then, did *Emma*, Jane's next novel, come to be dedicated to this man?

Henry became ill while he was negotiating with a new publisher, John Murray, founder of the influential *Quarterly Review*, who had agreed to publish *Emma*. Henry had refused Murray's offer to buy the copyrights of *Emma*, *Mansfield Park*, and *Sense and Sensibility* together for £450, thinking the offer was far too low, but after he became ill Jane agreed to have Murray publish *Emma* on commission—yes, again!

Henry, thankfully, would recover. One of the doctors who attended him was a court physician, who told Jane that the Prince was a great admirer of her work, with a set of her novels in each of his residences. Although those novels had been published anonymously, Jane's authorship was no longer a close secret by this time (and probably not one Henry would have kept from his doctors in any case). This doctor also informed the Prince that Miss Austen was in town. The result was that the Reverend James Stanier Clarke, the librarian of the Regent's lavish and grand Carlton House, visited her at Henry's and then invited her to visit Carlton

House in turn. It appears that during this visit Mr. Clarke suggested she might dedicate her next novel to the Prince Regent. Although Jane at first hesitated to do so, she soon understood that she had received a command. Her simple, restrained dedication was reworded by Murray into something as opulent as Carlton House itself:

TO

HIS ROYAL HIGHNESS

THE PRINCE REGENT,

THIS WORK IS,

BY HIS ROYAL HIGHNESS'S PERMISSION,

MOST RESPECTFULLY

DEDICATED,

BY HIS ROYAL HIGHNESS'S

DUTIFUL

AND OBEDIENT

HUMBLE SERVANT,

THE AUTHOR.

In a compliment to the dedication, Murray now hurried the proofs along and had them carried back and forth to Jane by the printer's boys. He also printed 2,000 copies of *Emma*, Jane's largest print run yet.

Jane Austen heard no specific opinion about the content of *Emma* from the Regent but received from Mr. Clarke "the Thanks of His Royal Highness the Prince Regent for the handsome Copy you sent him of your last excellent Novel." Jane tartly wrote to her publisher, "Whatever he may think of *my* share of the work, *Yours* seems to have been quite right." Jane's connection with Mr. Clarke was not yet at an end: As we shall see, it would take her into some wonderfully absurd new territory.

45 HINTS FROM VARIOUS QUARTERS

Reverend Clarke grew quite interested in Jane Austen: In addition to his official business with her concerning the dedication of *Emma* to the Prince Regent, he pursued a personal concern most energetically. The exchange of letters between Mr. Clarke and Jane at this time is wonderful. Mr. Clarke warmly expresses his own admiration of Jane's work and then suggests that her next novel should be a study of a clergyman "Fond of, & entirely engaged in Literature." No doubt Mr. Clarke had himself in mind as a model! Jane politely declines, thanking him graciously for the praise but pleading her poor education as an excuse. Because she has not had a classical education she could not possibly do justice to such a character. She is, she says, "the most unlearned, & uninformed Female who ever dared to be an Authoress."

Mr. Clarke is undeterred, however, and writes again, conceding that she might write about whatever kind of clergyman she likes. He helpfully suggests that she might show "what good would be done if Tythes were taken away entirely" and "describe him burying his own mother—as I did—because the High Priest of the Parish in which she died—did not pay her remains the respect he ought to do." From this outrage, Clarke writes solemnly, "I have never recovered the Shock." This clergyman Jane might write about should also go to sea—as, it happens, did Mr. Clarke himself. Imagine Jane's amusement and wonder growing with each line of his letter!

When Reverend Clarke conveys to Jane the thanks of the Prince Regent for the copy of *Emma* that was sent to him, he cannot resist another helpful hint, despite the lack of success he has had with his previous efforts. Next time, he writes, "you may chuse to dedicate your Volumes to Prince Leopold: any Historical Romance illustrative of the History of the august house of Cobourg, would just now be very interesting." As it happens, Clarke has "just now" been appointed chaplain and private English secretary to Prince Leopold (of Saxe-Cobourg), who is about to marry Princess Charlotte, so no doubt the subject does appear interesting to him. As James-Edward Austen-Leigh says, this "must have struck her as ludicrous," but, once again, she replies most civilly. Despite their absurdity, there is something sweet and touching about Mr. Clarke's letters, and Jane is unfailingly polite to him. But she stands her ground: "I could not sit seriously down to write a serious Romance under any other motive than to save my Life, & if it were indispensable for me to keep it up & never relax into laughing at myself or other people, I am sure I should be hung before I had finished the first Chapter.—No—I must keep to my own style & go on in my own Way."

This exchange of letters is entertaining enough on its own, but it also inspired the very funny "Plan of a Novel, According to Hints from Various Quarters," in which Austen "plans" a novel containing precisely the kind of absurdly unrealistic characters and plot developments she does not use in her own fiction. The heroine is "a faultless Character" and the daughter of a clergyman who, in following the outlines Mr. Clarke has supplied, is wonderfully ridiculous. Austen mercilessly incorporates Mr. Clarke's suggestions verbatim in some places, so that when her clergyman is about to die, having fled with his daughter to Kamchatka (in remotest eastern Asia) he, "after 4 or 5 hours of tender advice & parental Admonition to his miserable Child, expires in a fine burst of Literary Enthusiasm, intermingled with Invectives again(st) Holder's of Tythes."

The hero of this novel too will be "all perfection of course." Austen touches a theme we've seen before in her work: "All the Good will be unexceptionable in every respect—and there will be no foibles or weaknesses but with the Wicked, who will be completely depraved & infamous, hardly a resemblance of Humanity left in them." But as we know, thankfully, that is not Austen's "own style." In fact, one cannot find a single character who even comes close to this description in *Emma*, the novel that drew Jane Austen into this delightful correspondence with Reverend J. S. Clarke.

46 Who was Martha Lloyd and why did she live with Jane?

Martha Lloyd, who lived with Jane Austen for so many years, was the sister of Mary Lloyd, the second wife of Jane's brother James. The Lloyds moved into the parsonage at nearby Deane (where Mr. Austen was also the rector) in the spring of 1789, when Jane Austen was thirteen and living in Steventon. Martha's and Mary's sister was married to one of the Fowles, who were the Lloyds' cousins. The Fowle boys had attended the Austens' school, and Tom Fowle would become engaged to Cassandra Austen, so we can see that there were close connections between the Lloyds and Austens. In 1792, when James needed the Deane house for his first bride, Anne Mathew, the Lloyds moved to Ibthorpe, eighteen miles away. This was an inconvenient distance for young girls to travel, but Jane and Cassandra would now stay over when they visited the Lloyds. The friendship between Martha and both Austen girls had evidently taken deep root, and it would remain strong throughout their lives.

Martha was six years older than her sister Mary and ten years older than Jane, so Mary might seem the more logical choice for a friend, but Jane preferred the elder sister. Jane's cousin Eliza thought Martha "neither rich nor handsome," and both she and Mary had been scarred by smallpox, but Jane evidently found much in her to love. It seems Martha had a good sense of humor: Jane dedicated *Frederic and Elfrida*, one of her hilarious early writings, to her, and they shared many other jokes over the years. In a letter to Cassandra, written when Jane was twenty-three, Jane tells her sister how she and Martha stayed over at James's house after attending a ball, the two young women sharing a bed and lying awake talking until two in the morning. "I love Martha better than ever," Jane writes.

Throughout her letters Jane expresses great affection for, comfort with, and gratitude toward Martha, "the friend and sister under every circumstance." We know how trusted a confidante Martha must have been when we read Jane's joking reference to her having read *First Impressions* (*Pride and Prejudice*) so often that she could publish it from memory. This good friend also helped Jane go through Mr. Austen's books once the family had decided to leave Steventon and move to Bath.

Martha joined the Austens in Bath after her mother died. When Mrs. Austen, Jane, and Cassandra subsequently moved to Southampton, Martha was part of the household and would remain part of it until long after Jane's death. In Southampton, Martha and Jane went to the theater together, and attended a ball at the Dolphin, a night about which Jane wrote to Cassandra: "It was the same room in which we danced 15 years ago!—I thought it all over—& inspite of the shame of being so much older, felt with thankfulness that I was quite as happy now as then."

Jane would grow even happier with the move to Chawton Cottage, where Martha would of course move also. As we've seen, Martha apparently did some of the cooking at Chawton, and her book of recipes has survived to give us a glimpse into the meals she helped prepare.

Martha Lloyd's story has a very surprising ending: Frank Austen's wife Mary died in 1823 giving birth to her eleventh child, just as Edward's wife Elizabeth had died giving birth to *her* eleventh child. Frank, closest to Jane in age, was only fifty-four when, in 1828, he asked the sixty-three-year-old "spinster" Martha to become his second wife. Aunt Leigh-Perrot was scandalized by this marriage and decided not to leave Frank her house, as she had been considering. She did, however, leave him the grand sum of £10,000, with which he bought his own home, Portsdown House. There Cassandra sometimes visited her brother and her dear friend, now man and wife—Martha, as Cassandra said, making an excellent mother to his younger children. Frank was knighted for his long years of fine service in the Royal Navy, and so Martha, after an almost lifelong intimacy with the Austen family, would end her days as Lady Austen. She died in 1843, leaving Admiral Sir Francis Austen a widower again.

47 LONDON

Although Jane Austen criticized cities, both seriously and facetiously, in her novels and letters, on at least some occasions she certainly seems to have enjoyed London, that "Scene of Dissipation & vice." In particular, her visits to her favorite brother, Henry, and his wife, Jane's good friend Eliza, afforded her a great deal of pleasure.

At the time of Reverend George Austen's death in 1805, Henry and Eliza were living on Upper Berkeley Street, off Portman Square in London. Eliza, remember, had received a fortune from her godfather Warren Hastings, so they were living quite well, with a carriage and a French chef. At this time Henry, having left the militia, was a banker. Although Eliza's sickly son Hastings had died in 1801 at the young age of fifteen, his French nurse, Madame Bigeon, and her daughter, Madame Perigord, had become so attached to the family that they stayed on even after his death, and were also part of the household. Henry and Eliza were both the type better suited to the excitement and variety of the city than were the other Austens.

Later, after they had moved to a small house in Brompton, just outside the city, Jane visited them there and enjoyed a quite different lifestyle from the one she knew in the country or in the homes of her other brothers. Since Henry and Eliza had no children now that Hastings was gone, conversation was pretty much focused on adult matters. The household was cultured and sophisticated: Henry and Eliza attended plays, concerts, and the opera, where Henry had his own box. They visited museums. Jane too took part in all these pursuits during her visits. She also enjoyed the company of the Frenchwomen Madame Bigeon and Madame Perigord, who were pretty much part of the family by now.

In the spring of 1811, with Henry and Eliza now living on Sloane Street in town, Jane stayed with them while correcting proofs of *Sense and Sensibility*. The proofs were slow in coming, and Henry was trying to hurry the printer. He and Eliza threw a musical party with more than sixty guests, as Jane recounts in a letter to Cassandra. There were hired pianists, harpists, and singers, as well as rented decorations. Jane thought the music "extremely good." The London homes of Henry and Eliza consistently afforded Jane special pleasures and unique opportunities—like this one— for observing people. As Elizabeth Bennet rightly notes, there are "not such a variety of people to be met with in the country as in town."

After Eliza's death in 1813, Jane continued to visit Henry in London, still taking advantage of its cultural resources and its pretty parks and gardens. She wrote happily about one of her visits: "I liked my solitary elegance very much, & was ready to laugh all the time, at my being where I was.—I could not but feel that I had naturally small right to be parading about London in a Barouche [Edward's luxurious open carriage]."

Although there might be occasions when town struck Jane as offering "plenty of mortar & nothing to do," in her visits to her brother Henry's she clearly found plenty to do, and plenty to enjoy in London.

48 MRS. AUSTEN: WHAT WAS JANE'S MOTHER LIKE?

If a person has heard anything at all about Jane Austen's mother, it is probably that she was a hypochondriac. That seems to be true, but there is much more to be told about Mrs. Austen, the intriguing woman with whom Jane lived her entire life.

As we've seen, Cassandra Leigh, after whom Jane's sister was named, was the daughter of the Reverend Thomas Leigh. Mrs. Austen's father was a scholar, as was her uncle, Theophilus Leigh, whom she impressed with her precocious intelligence as a child. James-Edward Austen-Leigh notes that Theophilus was "a man more famous for his sayings than his doings, overflowing with puns and witticisms and sharp retorts." After giving examples of the Master's wit, Austen-Leigh naturally concludes his description of the gentleman: "I do not know from what common ancestor the Master of Balliol and his great-niece Jane Austen, with some others of the family, may have derived the keen sense of humour which they certainly possessed." Mrs. Austen combined this keen sense of humor with a lively imagination and a good deal of common sense.

For all her aristocratic and scholarly background, Mrs. Austen's practical streak and lack of concern with appearances served her well as the wife of a country clergyman and farmer with a very modest income. She jokes in a letter to her sister-in-law, after saying how she would like to show off her children, that she would like to show off her other "riches" too—her bull, cows, ducks, and chickens.

She was not only a mother to eight children of her own; she also seems to have done quite well mothering her husband's pupils firmly but fairly, looking after their meals and laundry and their characters, too. Mrs. Austen wrote poetry from childhood on, and we have some of her very clever light verse, including the poems she regularly wrote to these boys. The verses are charming and spirited—and often relayed a specific message—and evidently meant enough to her charges that they preserved them their whole lives, so that we can enjoy them today.

Like so many women in Jane Austen's novels, Mrs. Austen was a strong, confident woman. She could be stubborn, and she sometimes made tart remarks about the neighbors—as did Jane (in private, of course). Even after she fell seriously ill in Bath, she recovered to write a cheerful, defiant poem called "Dialogue between Death & Mrs. Austen."

Once Mr. and Mrs. Austen moved to Bath, the pair enjoyed that city as well as the excursions they took to various resorts. After she was widowed, Mrs. Austen took pleasure in visiting her relatives, taking along her daughters. At Stoneleigh Abbey she counted the windows (forty-five) and described the grand rooms with enthusiasm and a novelist's imagination and eye for detail.

Once Mrs. Austen was settled at Chawton Cottage with her daughters and Martha Lloyd, she especially enjoyed working in the garden. Her favorite grandchild, Anna, recalls how she delighted in the vegetable and flower gardens both, digging up her own potatoes. Caroline Austen recalls how her grandmother loved to sit in the dining room with her needlework or writing. That was the room that looked out on the main road, and she enjoyed the "stirring scene" outside the window. We also see how much she enjoyed reading Jane's novels.

From these various accounts we get a picture of a very strong character. Jane could sometimes get irritated with her mother, but, as with her brother James, the other writer in the family, it may be that certain similarities in their personalities caused this friction. And, as also with James, there is no doubt that the love between Jane and Mrs. Austen was strong.

49 JANE AUSTEN, POET

Like Mrs. Austen, Jane Austen also wrote poetry on occasion. We have seen that she wrote a moving elegy on the death of her good friend Mrs. Lefroy. But most of her verse—again, she is taking after her mother—was comic or celebratory. Although these poems are well done, Jane obviously did not consider herself a serious poet in the way her brother James thought of himself at one time.

One of Jane's poems is a lovely celebration of her brother Frank's wedding. She sent it to her niece Fanny because it was written for her too—it is in her voice, as if she is excitedly welcoming her uncle and his new bride to Godmersham. It is charming and paints a joyous picture of the occasion.

Frank provides the inspiration for another poem, too. Upon the birth of his second child—his first son—Jane sent him a congratulatory poem in which she hopes the child inherits all his father's traits, including the fiery daring and "insolence of spirit" Frank displayed even in the nursery. Again, Jane paints a picture of the scene and, as in the previous poem, includes direct speech (betraying her novelist's impulses). Little Frank's boldness is tempered in the poem by his sweet assurance to his nurse that he is not really being disobedient. Jane vividly conveys the sense of her brother's energy, even as a little boy.

Jane wrote an amusing poem in mock praise of her niece Anna, which includes these lines:

> Her wit descends on foes and friends
>   Like famed Niagara's Fall;
> And travellers gaze in wild amaze,
>   And listen, one and all.
> Her judgment sound, thick, black, profound,
>   Like transatlantic groves,
> Dispenses aid, and friendly shade
>   To all that in it roves.

James-Edward Austen-Leigh, Anna's half-brother, remarks that Jane basically wrote this poem off the top of her head.

Many of Austen's short humorous poems contain riddles and other wordplay. The Austens sometimes passed the time by collaborating on such poems for their own amusement. Jane Austen, in her life and in her work, was always finding entertainment in language games, and this particular kind of playfulness seems to have been a family trait.

50 WAS JANE AUSTEN A SNOB?

Yes, Jane Austen was a snob, but not about class, title, or wealth. She was a snob about intellect, thoughtfulness, and manners. We've seen that her mother was proud of her ancestry: She was descended from a sixteenth-century Lord Mayor of London and named for the wife of a great-uncle who became Duke of Chandos. Because her sons could claim status as "Founder's Kin," they were awarded scholarships to St. John's College, Oxford. In light of the grandeur of Mrs. Austen's ancestry, it's interesting to see that she sent her children out to be brought up in the humblest of surroundings. The cottage where each child was nursed by a foster mother was, as James-Edward Austen-Leigh writes, "home, and must have remained so until [the child] was old enough to run about and talk." The Steventon parsonage was modest enough—the Austens might not have had much money, but Mr. Austen was an Oxford-educated clergyman and a gentleman—but a village cottage was on another level of gentility altogether!

If Mrs. Austen's snobbishness was somewhat theoretical and not much seen in practice by her children, Jane did get a good dose of it at her brother Edward's grand estate in Kent, Godmersham. Although Jane was of course loved by the family, she apparently was treated with some condescension there. She in turn wasn't much impressed by the gentry who visited. Although there was no denying she found Godmersham luxurious—who wouldn't?—her letters show that she could be bored there in the wrong company. The company she preferred, apart from that of her nieces and nephews, was that of the governess, Anne Sharp.

Anne Sharp was a clever, hardworking woman in a position that in *Emma* is compared by Jane Fairfax to the slave trade. She would remain one of Jane's closest friends even after leaving Godmersham in 1806. We've seen how Jane also befriended the two Frenchwomen who stayed on in Henry and Eliza's household after the death of young Hastings. It is clear that Jane Austen chose friends with no regard to their social status. How is social status treated in her novels?

Lady Catherine de Bourgh in *Pride and Prejudice* is quite preoccupied with the subject of rank. As she tells Elizabeth Bennet: "My daughter and my nephew are formed for each other. They are descended on the maternal side, from the same noble line; and, on the father's, from respectable, honourable, and ancient, though untitled families." She dismisses what she calls the "upstart pretensions of a young woman without family, connections, or fortune." Elizabeth Bennet rejects all her arguments as "frivolous," which is a politer term than they deserve.

In *Persuasion*, Sir Walter Elliot is even more harshly portrayed for his pride in and fascination with his own rank and ancestry. This obsession is given the important first line of the novel, and it fixes his character: "Sir Walter Elliot, of Kellynch-hall, in Somersetshire, was a man who, for his own amusement, never took up any book but the Baronetage." That is a double whammy if ever there was one—a snob who never reads novels! Later on in the book he and his daughter Elizabeth will show that they may have vanity but no real pride when they betray great eagerness to be recognized by the Dowager Viscountess Dalrymple and her daughter, the Honourable Miss Carteret, noble cousins who are, in the heroine Anne's view, "nothing": "There was no superiority of manner, accomplishment, or understanding." These are what would impress Anne.

Snobbishness is the flaw of the entire Elliot family with the exception of Anne. Even Anne's otherwise superior mother, Lady Elliot, had been infatuated by rank, and Lady Russell, Anne's friend and adviser, "had prejudices on the side of ancestry; she had a value for rank and consequence, which blinded her a little to the faults of those who possessed them." It also blinded her to the value of Captain Wentworth, who did not possess them.

Lord Osborne in *The Watsons*, though a lord, is quite foolish and arrogant. Emma Woodhouse is punished for her snobbishness regarding her friendly neighbors, the Coles. Many more examples can be found to demonstrate that in her life and in her writing, Jane Austen shows her contempt for judgments of people based upon considerations such as ancestry and wealth rather than individual merit.

51 "WHAT HAVE WEALTH OR GRANDEUR TO DO WITH HAPPINESS?"

The question of the importance of money in Jane Austen's life and her novels is a different issue from that of the importance of social position. The two very often did not go together: Someone might have a title and no money, or money and no title. Indeed, often those with titles were on a mission to marry into wealth. We have seen what Jane Austen thought of social rank. How did she feel about money?

The title question here is asked rhetorically by Marianne in *Sense and Sensibility*. Her sensible sister Elinor responds to it: "Grandeur has but little . . . but wealth has much to do with it." Marianne, the romantic sister, scolds Elinor for this response, but Elinor is not greedy or mercenary, simply so practical-minded that when she and Edward Ferrars finally come to an understanding at the end of the novel, " . . . they were neither of them quite enough in love to think that three hundred and fifty pounds a-year would supply them with the comforts of life." Marianne would like to think of herself as being able to "exist on Love," but she also makes provisions in her fantasy for a "proper establishment of servants, a carriage, perhaps two, and hunters [horses]."

Although Elizabeth Bennet jokes that she can date her love of Mr. Darcy to her "first seeing his beautiful grounds at Pemberley," she is truly not mercenary. She turns down one proposal from Darcy and we see her attitude toward wealth again in regard to his aunt, Lady Catherine de Bourgh: "She had heard nothing of Lady Catherine that spoke her awful [that is, awesome] from any extraordinary talents or miraculous virtue, and the mere stateliness of money and rank, she thought she could witness without trepidation." Although Elizabeth isn't herself impressed by wealth, she is willing to excuse Mr. Wickham's "prudence" in seeking to marry a woman he doesn't love, simply for her money. Elizabeth tells her aunt coolly that "handsome young men must have something to live on, as well as the plain." It is simply the way of the world. Later, though, she will be ashamed of herself for having been so wrong as to excuse such "hatefully" mercenary motives.

In *Mansfield Park*, Maria Bertram is planning to marry Mr. Rushworth only because he is very rich. Her brother Edmund is the only one in the family to disapprove: "He could allow his sister to be the best judge of her own happiness, but he was not pleased that her happiness should centre in a large income; nor could he refrain from often saying to himself, in Mr. Rushworth's company, 'If this man had not twelve thousand a year, he would be a very stupid fellow.'" Maria sets herself up for disaster with this move, and she is severely punished at the end of the novel for it. In this novel in particular, mercenary motives are analyzed and condemned. Naive young Catherine Morland says quite rightly in *Northanger Abbey*, "To marry for money I think the wickedest thing in existence" and Austen never departs from that view.

Still, in her own life Jane Austen found having no money—in our terms—a real drag. She didn't lack the bare necessities of life—food, shelter, clothing, and even what we might consider luxuries, such as a piano or a servant—but for most of her life she had no money at all of her own, and so was entirely dependent on her family for everything she needed or wanted. She had to go along with the choices others made for her concerning where she would live. She couldn't move freely from place to place because, of course, she had no means of transportation of her own. We know she was sometimes distressed by the fact that her little plans always depended on the accommodation of others, who might have different ideas. And we've seen how Jane was unable to buy *Northanger Abbey* back from the publisher for £10. As Emma Watson tells Lord Osborne when he suggests that women can always find the money to do what they want to do: "Female economy will do a great deal my Lord, but it cannot turn a small income into a large one."

But as that same Emma Watson also says, "Poverty is a great evil, but to a woman of education and feeling it ought not, it cannot be the greatest." Happily, Jane Austen eventually found a way to make some money: through her writing. Considering that we are talking about the greatest novels ever written, she didn't make much, but even a little was enough to give her a bit of independence. She was able to give presents, which clearly delighted her: "Do not refuse me," she tells Cass after sending her a gift of dress material, "I am very rich."

So while Jane Austen certainly understood the value of money and knew what it had to do with happiness, she—and all her heroines—clearly held other things in much greater esteem.

52 "OH! WHAT A HENRY."

Caroline Austen writes of her aunt that she "was a very affectionate sister to all her Brothers—One of them in particular was her especial pride and delight." That was Henry Austen, the fourth son. Caroline's brother James-Edward Austen-Leigh writes that Henry "had great conversational powers, and inherited from his father an eager and sanguine disposition. He was a very entertaining companion, but had perhaps less steadiness of purpose, certainly less success in life, than his brothers." Henry was by all accounts a charmer, his father's favorite as well as Jane's. After remarking to Cassandra that she has just had an entertaining letter from him, Jane adds, "there is no merit to him in *that*, he cannot help being amusing."

With such a personality, Henry no doubt performed with spirit in the family theatricals at Steventon, where he flirted with his then-married cousin Eliza, whom he would later marry. Before Eliza accepted his second proposal, however, he was engaged to another woman. Henry always claimed that Mary Pearson was the one who ended that engagement, but with Henry you have to wonder about the circumstances. Like James, Henry attended Oxford University, and he contributed pieces to James's magazine, *The Loiterer*. He served as an officer in the Oxford Militia during the war with France, for which he gave up his plan to be ordained. It seems that Henry was attracted to livelier occupations than that of clergyman, at least as a young man.

After leaving the militia, Henry Austen set himself up as a banker. He and Eliza seemed to be living well in London at the time of Mr. Austen's death, yet he pleaded his "present precarious income" when offering to chip in £50 per year to help support his mother and sisters.

Whatever his income, he loved visiting his brother Edward's grand estate Godmersham, and he frequently did so without his wife. He probably felt it was the kind of life that suited him best, since he had the taste and abilities to appreciate it. Being a very entertaining companion for adults and children alike, he was always most welcome there.

As we've seen, Henry assisted Jane a great deal with the publication of her novels, and Eliza helped too. When Eliza died in 1813, Jane noted of her brother, "his Mind is not a Mind for affliction." Indeed, before long he was involved with several new women.

In 1816, Henry's bank crashed and Henry was declared bankrupt. His uncle James Leigh-Perrot and brother Edward had guaranteed the very large amounts of £10,000 and £20,000, which they then lost, and others in the family lost smaller amounts, including even Jane, who lost £13. She refers to the bankruptcy in a letter as "the late sad Event in Henrietta St." Despite the hardship Henry's failure caused them, the Austen family drew loyally together as always and supported him. Henry himself, resilient as ever, remained cheerful, and he was not blamed for the trouble the collapse of his bank caused the Austens. Now, at long last, Henry decided to become a priest after all, and was ordained.

You wonder if Henry was in part the inspiration for some of those lively, charming male characters in Jane's novels, some of whom are also named Henry—Henry Tilney and Henry Crawford—as well as George Wickham and Frank Churchill. With the exception of Henry Tilney, these characters also lack "steadiness of purpose," which makes falling for them—despite their charm—a risky proposition indeed.

53 SISTERS-IN-LAW

Jane Austen had just one sister, Cassandra, who, although older than Jane, would survive her. Her sisters-in-law were another story, and Jane watched as, one after another, the wives of her brothers met an early death.

The eldest Austen son, James, married Anne Mathew, who was a little older than he was, tall and slender with beautiful dark eyes. Her father, General Edward Mathew, had fought against the Americans and was later made governor of Grenada. Some serious financial trouble in Anne's family related to her father's service to the Crown would have a severe adverse effect on James also. Anne gave birth to Jane Anna Elizabeth, known as Anna, in April 1793. Almost exactly two years later, Anne died suddenly at home. The doctor diagnosed it as probably a ruptured liver. Anne Austen was in her mid-thirties when she died. James would take Mary Lloyd, Martha's sister, as his second wife.

As we've seen, Edward Austen's wife Elizabeth died at the age of thirty-five after giving birth to her eleventh child (and Frank's wife Mary would share the same fate, though not until after Jane's death). Pretty and elegant Elizabeth, the daughter of a Kentish baronet, had married at eighteen and spent the remaining years of her life as a devoted wife and mother. Anna, the daughter of James and Anne, later said that she didn't think Elizabeth had been very fond of Jane or "at least that she very much preferred the elder Sister. A little talent went a long way with the Goodneston Bridgeses of that period; & *much* must have gone a long way too far." It is unusual to hear that anyone preferred Cassandra's company to Jane's.

Then there was Henry's wife Eliza, of course, with whom Jane was very close. Eliza died at the age of fifty-one, probably of breast cancer, the same disease that had killed her mother, Mr. Austen's sister. According to the accounts of Jane and Henry both, Eliza endured a long, painful illness before dying in the spring of 1813. In 1820 Henry married again, this time a woman named Miss Eleanor Jackson, about whom not much has been recorded.

The baby of the family, Charles Austen, married seventeen-year-old Fanny Palmer in Bermuda while he was serving in the Royal Navy. Fanny bore Charles three daughters and then died after giving birth to a fourth girl. The baby died a few weeks later. Fanny Austen was only twenty-four years old.

54 "A VERY MUSICAL SOCIETY"
In addition to being a great writer, Jane Austen had another artistic talent that was an important aspect of her life: She was also a good musician. She might have begun with piano lessons at Mrs. La Tournelle's Abbey School. Later she was taught by George Chard, the assistant organist at Winchester Cathedral. Caroline Austen writes of the daily routine at Chawton Cottage: "Aunt Jane began her day with music—for which I

conclude she had a natural taste; as she thus kept it up—tho' she had no one to teach; was never induced (as I have heard) to play in company; and none of her family cared much for it." Caroline recounts how as a child she enjoyed listening to her aunt, and describes how Jane would play from music she had copied out herself "so neatly and correctly, that it was as easy to read as print." (Printed music was very expensive, so Jane made copies of borrowed music.) Caroline's brother James-Edward also remarks on their aunt's sweet voice, and recalls the "simple old songs" she would sing while accompanying herself on the piano. Apparently she was especially fond of tender love songs.

Jane didn't have a piano in any of the Bath residences, but she did rent one for the Castle Square house in Southampton with money from her very modest allowance. And the purchase of a piano was immediately part of the Chawton plan: "Yes, yes, we *will* have a Pianoforte, as good a one as can be got for 30 Guineas." Jane promises to practice country dances, such as Mrs. Weston in *Emma* excels in.

Jane Austen's novels are full of music. It is amusing to note how she gives Catherine Morland in *Northanger Abbey* quite a different "natural taste" from her own: after a year of piano lessons she "could not bear it" and "The day which dismissed the music-master was one of the happiest of Catherine's life." Fanny Price does not play either, but she has taste enough to appreciate Mary Crawford's enchanting performance on the harp, perceiving the "superior tone and expression" of her rival's playing.

Music makes several appearances in *Pride and Prejudice*. We are told that Elizabeth Bennet's "performance was pleasing, though by no means capital." Her sister Mary has worked much harder at her music, but unfortunately she "had neither genius nor taste; and though vanity had given her application, it had given her likewise a pedantic air and conceited manner, which would have injured a higher degree of excellence than she had reached. Elizabeth, easy and unaffected, had been listened to with much more pleasure, though not playing half so well." No doubt the author is giving her own opinion based on her experience of hearing many musical performances. And in the same novel Lady Catherine makes this wonderfully absurd boast: "There are few people in England, I suppose, who have more true enjoyment of music than myself, or a better natural taste. If I had ever learnt, I should have been a great proficient."

In *Emma*, Jane Fairfax's superb playing and singing are a source of irritation to Austen's heroine. After a night when the two had both performed in public, Emma "did unfeignedly and unequivocally regret the inferiority of her own playing and singing. She did most heartily grieve over the idleness of her childhood—and sat down and practised vigorously an hour and a half." It's interesting to see how Austen endows both Elizabeth and Emma with only middling musical skills, though like Elizabeth, Emma "wanted neither taste nor spirit" in her playing and "could accompany her own voice well."

Music is very often used for comic purposes in the novels, but in *Persuasion* we find something else. When dancing is proposed at the end of a lively evening at Uppercross, Anne Elliot chooses to play for the others rather than dance herself, "though her eyes would sometimes fill with tears as she sat at the instrument." When Captain Wentworth inquires of someone else whether Anne never dances, the sad answer is "Oh! no, never; she has quite given up dancing. She had rather play." Music is used to convey meaning in another way too: Anne tries to give Captain Wentworth encouragement about her feelings—which she cannot express directly—when she urges him to stay for the rest of a concert: "'Is not this song worth staying for?' said Anne. . . . 'No!' he replied impressively, 'there is nothing worth my staying for;' and he was gone directly." And the strength of his negative response to a question apparently about a song assures Anne that he still loves her.

55 DRAWING

Jane Austen's nephew tells us that when *Sense and Sensibility* was published, some people thought the sisters Elinor and Marianne represented Cassandra and Jane. Marianne, like Jane, played the piano. However, James-Edward Austen-Leigh is surely right in saying that his aunt was emphatically not Marianne, who, again, "spent whole hours at the pianoforté alternately singing and crying; her voice often totally suspended by her tears." That could hardly be Jane Austen! He concedes, though, that Cassandra, the calmer and more prudent of the two, might have been represented by Elinor's sensible character. Another similarity is that Cassandra, like Elinor, liked to draw. In fact, Cassandra drew the only portraits we have of Jane, one of which we have discussed. The other is—frustratingly—a back view. The samples of her work that have survived show that Jane's sister was a good artist.

In several of the novels, including *Sense and Sensibility*, Jane Austen playfully brings in contemporary aesthetic principles, in particular the theory of the picturesque as it was codified by William Gilpin. In *Northanger Abbey* Henry and Eleanor Tilney view the country around Bath "with the eyes of persons accustomed to drawing," and Catherine Morland is ashamed that she cannot understand them. But this is one of the rare instances when the Tilneys are themselves being gently satirized, for embracing a trendy theory and its jargon. Catherine's "ignorance" in this case is equally the common sense that sees that the emperor is not wearing clothes: "It seemed as if a good view were no longer to be taken from the top of an high hill, and that a clear blue sky was no longer a proof of a fine day." After Henry's lecture to Catherine on the picturesque, however, "she voluntarily rejected the whole city of Bath, as unworthy to make part of a landscape."

Edward Ferrars reflects Catherine's pre-education taste when he says to Marianne,

> *"Remember I have no knowledge in the picturesque, and I shall offend you by my ignorance and want of taste if we come to particulars. I shall call hills steep, which ought to be bold; surfaces strange and uncouth, which ought to be irregular and rugged; and distant objects out of sight, which ought only to be indistinct. . . . I like a fine prospect, but not on picturesque principles. I do not like crooked, twisted, blasted trees. I admire them much more if they are tall, straight and flourishing."*

Elinor and Edward gang up on Marianne to mock her "passion for dead leaves," but Austen manages to have it both ways, making fun of the perversity of much romantic art and artistic theory generally while at the same time presenting Marianne's passion as very attractive. Henry Austen said that Jane liked Gilpin, but she ridicules the pretentious talk of his followers, who use language that has become, in Marianne's words, "a mere jargon": "Every body pretends to feel and tries to describe with the taste and elegance of him who first defined what picturesque beauty was." Austen suggests that while it might be perverse to reject blue skies and straight trees and the whole city of Bath on aesthetic principle, it is also possible to be too prosaically sensible when it come to nature and art both. Romantic dead leaves, ruins, and crooked trees *are* beautiful, and they are worthy objects for an artist.

Austen uses drawing in a totally different comic vein in *Emma*. Emma possesses a talent for drawing on a par with her talent for music. She "had made more progress both in drawing and music than many might have done with so little labour as she would ever submit to. She played and sang;—and drew in almost every style; but steadiness had always been wanting; and in nothing had she approached the degree of excellence which she would have been glad to command, and ought not to have failed of."

Emma has begun many portraits but finished not one. She does finish a watercolor portrait of Harriet, however, and in the responses of various characters to it we see the essence of each personality. Mrs. Weston, Emma's former governess and indulgent friend, finds that Emma has corrected the only flaw in Harriet's face. Mr. Elton, the eager, presumptuous clergyman, gushes over the portrait without regard for either taste or truth: "It appears to me a most perfect resemblance in every feature. I never saw such a likeness in my life. We must allow for the effect of shade, you know." Mr. Knightley, who always tells Emma the truth in the plainest English, says bluntly, "You have made her too tall, Emma." Emma denies this though she knows it's true. Finally, Mr. Woodhouse praises the portrait as "very pretty" and adds, "The only thing I do not thoroughly like is, that she seems to be sitting out of doors, with only a little shawl over her shoulders—and it makes one think she must catch cold." As always, Mr. Woodhouse leaves the real world—in this case the portrait—behind and leads us into the world of obsession in his head.

56 "A CURRICLE WAS THE PRETTIEST EQUIPAGE IN THE WORLD": HORSES AND CARRIAGES

Modes of transportation are important in Jane Austen's writings going all the way back to the juvenilia. Young Jane would have listened in on a lot of talk about horses and carriages from all those boys living in the house. Just as young men today can become obsessed with cars and motorcycles, some of Austen's male characters are rather too interested in their carriages.

John Thorpe, in *Northanger Abbey*, is an example of such a character. He incessantly brags about his horse (whose speed and spirit he exaggerates to impress Catherine and instead only alarms her) and his "gig." A gig was an open light vehicle drawn by one horse. Often the gig had a top that could be lowered—a "convertible." It could be sporty and was often driven in Austen's novels by young men. Here is John Thorpe describing his: "Curricle-hung you see; seat, trunk, sword-case, splashing-board, lamps, silver moulding, all you see complete; the iron-work as good as new, or better." In this gig he will carry Catherine off in a mock abduction.

John Thorpe's gig would have been inferior to a curricle, which was the real "sports car" of carriages. It was similar to a gig, but because it was drawn by two horses, it was faster and even more dangerous. The seats on both of these carriages were very high and the vehicles were quick to overturn. (Jane's cousin Eliza remarked on the risk she took in trusting her neck to Henry's coachmanship.) The title quotation here is from Catherine Morland, who happily has a rather better experience in Henry Tilney's curricle: "Henry drove so well,—so quietly—without making any disturbance. . . . And then his hat sat so well, and the innumerable capes of his greatcoat looked so becomingly important!–To be driven by him, next to being dancing with him, was certainly the greatest happiness in the world." This is also Marianne's feeling when Willoughby drives her about Allenham in *his* curricle in *Sense and Sensibility*. Mr. Darcy drives a curricle, as do William Elliot and Charles Musgrove in *Persuasion*, the very wealthy Mr. Rushworth in *Mansfield Park*, and the rich, flirtatious, and popular Tom Musgrave in *The Watsons*. It was quite the dashing young man's vehicle of choice!

Although Catherine loves riding in Henry's curricle, alas, she is sent away from Northanger in a "hack post-chaise," a rented carriage. And, to add to the indignity, she will not even have a servant with her: "A journey of seventy miles, to be taken post by you, at your age, alone, unattended!" as Eleanor Tilney sums it up. Ladies did not travel unattended, and Catherine's trip was not a direct one, but was made in stages. As her mother says after she has arrived home safely, "you must have been forced to have your wits about you, with so much changing of chaises and so forth."

Jane Austen was only too aware of the dangers of horses and carriages. Both her cousin Jane Cooper and her friend Mrs. Lefroy were killed in accidents involving horses. The roads were very bad (talk about potholes!), the vehicles precarious, and, of course, the horses not always predictable.

Of course, gentlemen often simply rode their horses from place to place, as Jane Austen's brothers frequently did. In particular, James, the eldest, loved to ride about the countryside on horseback. Jane Bennet is the rare lady in Austen's novels to ride horseback, which is how she travels to Netherfield, although she would prefer the coach. But her mother has other ideas: "No, my dear, you had better go on horseback, because it seems likely to rain; and then you must stay all night." Ladies on horseback will actually be an important topic in *Mansfield Park*. Lord Osborne says to Emma Watson, "A woman never looks better than on horseback," but very few women in Austen's novels ride.

As for larger vehicles, the Bennets and Musgroves own coaches, which might have held four, six, or even more passengers. General Tilney travels in grand style with his chaise-and-four with liveried postilions, that is, riders on the horses rather than a seated driver.

In *Emma*, Mr. Knightley keeps no horses and, to Emma's disapproval, does "not use his carriage so often as became the owner of Donwell Abbey." She is a bit snobbish about such matters, but he does not share her concern for appearances.

Several of Austen's funniest uses of carriages appear in *Emma*. First there is the scene where Emma is forced into a tête-à-tête carriage ride with tipsy Mr. Elton, who, as soon as the door is shut on them, is "making violent love to her"—that is, declaring his love. To add to Emma's ridiculous predicament, the carriage must move at a snail's pace because of Mr. Woodhouse's fear about the snow. Later in the novel, Mr. Elton has found a different bride. Much to Emma's irritation, Mrs. Elton delights in bragging about her brother's high-end carriage, the magnificent and rare barouche-landau, "which holds four perfectly." The ordinary barouche was a four-horse vehicle owned by those in the higher social spheres. According to Edward Ratcliffe, it "has a folding top that covers only the back half of the passenger area," whereas "the barouche-landau top covers the entire passenger area when raised and is arranged in two parts: the front part folds forward, the back part folds to the rear." Finally, there is Frank Churchill's "extraordinary dream" about Mr. Perry's plan to set up his carriage, which Frank fabricates on the spot to cover up his blunder in letting slip a piece of gossip he actually heard from Jane Fairfax.

No doubt about it, horses and carriages were extremely important in Jane Austen's world.

57 JANE AUSTEN'S GARDENS

Jane Austen loved the country and much preferred living there to living in the city. One aspect of nature that interested her was not completely "natural," however, but was cultivated by human design and care: the garden. At Steventon, where she grew up, the rectory had "one of those old-fashioned gardens in which vegetables and flowers are combined," according to Jane's nephew. The garden contained, among other things, potatoes, strawberry beds, and a sundial. There were elm trees and hedgerows, with wildflowers contributing to the beauty of the scene: primroses, anemones, bluebells, and wild hyacinths.

In Bath Jane enjoyed the beautiful public gardens, but once in Southampton the gardener in her comes to life again with the anticipated move to the house in Castle Square. As she tells Cassandra,

> *Our Garden is putting in order. . . . The Shrubs which border the gravel walk [the gardener] says are only sweetbriar & roses, & the latter of an indifferent sort;—we mean to get a few of a better kind therefore, & at my own particular desire he procures us some Syringas. . . . We talk also of a Laburnum.—The border under the Terrace Wall, is clearing away to receive Currants & Gooseberry Bushes, & a spot is found very proper for Raspberries.*

This pleasant garden, which ran to the old city walls, seems to have been one of the things that made Jane happiest in the time spent between her homes in Steventon and Chawton.

In Chawton, the cheerful garden was Mrs. Austen's domain, while Jane had other things to occupy her—writing masterpieces. It is amusing to note that she makes a passion for gardening part of the character of one of the most repulsive and absurd characters in her fiction, Mr. Collins in *Pride and Prejudice*: "To work in his garden was one of his most respectable pleasures." His wife Charlotte encourages him in this pursuit, which is no doubt part of her plan to keep him away from her as much as possible: "When Mr. Collins could be forgotten, there was really a great air of comfort throughout [the parsonage], and by Charlotte's evident enjoyment of it, Elizabeth supposed he must be often forgotten." Alas, a passion for gardening does not necessarily reflect anything else good about a person's character.

58 "To be fond of dancing . . . "

"It may be possible to do without dancing entirely," wrote Jane Austen in *Emma*, but she clearly didn't believe that was true. She continues, "When the felicities of rapid motion have once been, though slightly, felt—it must be a very heavy set that does not ask for more." According to Henry Austen, Jane "was fond of dancing, and excelled in it." She gives the same love of dancing to her heroines. It was the most important social activity for young men and women. As a young woman Jane eagerly attended formal balls and, since she lived in the country, happily took part in informal, impromptu dancing with family and neighbors in the evening, where one of the older women present would oblige by sitting down at the piano.

While living at Steventon, Jane and Cassandra attended the assemblies at Basingstoke. Among other places, they also danced at the Dolphin Inn in Southampton, and we've seen how Jane danced there again fifteen years later, and assured Cassandra she was quite as happy as she had been at eighteen. Jane's earliest surviving letter relates to Cassandra her "profligate and shocking" behavior with Tom Lefroy at a ball. It was very indiscreet "*to be particular*" in such a setting as they were—but Jane rather proudly says others can take lessons from her in the subject. Balls were held on moonlit nights so drivers could see the roads for the trip home, but sometimes Jane would stay over at a friend's and lie awake talking over the evening, just as she would have plenty to say about balls she attended in her letters to Cassandra, describing precisely and entertainingly who did what with whom.

In *Northanger Abbey*, Catherine Morland is disappointed when she has no one to dance with at her first ball in Bath, but she soon finds a delightful partner in Henry Tilney. Afterward, she meets his sister: "'How well your brother dances!' was an artless exclamation of Catherine's towards the close of their conversation, which at once surprised and amused her companion." Skill in dancing appears to be a requisite trait for Austen's heroes. Mr. Darcy also dances well. Despite his own "superior dancing," he asserts rudely that "Every savage can dance." Perhaps, but Elizabeth Bennet's cousin Mr. Collins cannot: he, "awkward and solemn, apologising instead of attending, and often moving wrong without being aware of it, gave her [Elizabeth] all the shame and misery which a disagreeable partner for a couple of dances can give. The moment of her release from him was exstacy."

The ability to dance well is necessary to the character of a hero but not sufficient for one. In *Sense and Sensibility*, Sir John Middleton assures Marianne that Willoughby danced "from eight o'clock till four, without once sitting down." This knowledge makes Marianne's eyes sparkle and she is further assured, to her delight, that he did so "with elegance, with spirit." Marianne is impressed, but we know Willoughby is no hero!

In *Mansfield Park*, Fanny Price would not seem to have a character that takes pleasure in dancing, but even *she* comes to anticipate a ball with happy excitement. Indeed, "She had hardly ever been in a state so nearly approaching high spirits in her life." And the fact that Anne Elliot, at the beginning of *Persuasion*, has "'quite given up dancing'" is evidence of her broken heart and loss of interest in life. For Jane Austen, it would be unnatural for a young woman not to love to dance with an attractive partner at every opportunity. Even a female friend or a brother would do in a pinch, as long as they didn't dance like Mr. Collins! It was a single woman's most significant and effective means of exercise and release from tension and cares.

Mr. Knightley in *Emma* stands out among Austen's heroes as being "no dancer in general." But like so much in *Emma*, this is a sly deception because, just as Emma deduces from his walk "in how gentlemanlike a manner, with what natural grace, he must have danced, would he but take the trouble," his dancing in the next moment proves to be "extremely good." So taken is Emma with Mr. Knightley's kindness in asking Harriet to dance that she, in effect, asks *him* to dance:

> *"Whom are you going to dance with?" asked Mr. Knightley.*
> *She hesitated a moment, and then replied, "With you, if you will ask me."*

And of course he does!

As is the case with music, much meaning is conveyed through dancing in Jane Austen's novels, just as it was in her life.

PART 5

Heroes and Heroines

59 WHY ARE THERE SO MANY CLERGYMEN IN JANE AUSTEN'S NOVELS?

Jane Austen was the daughter and granddaughter of clergymen. Two of her brothers, James and Henry, were clergymen, as were her cousin Edward Cooper and Cassandra's fiancé, Tom Fowle. (Several of her nephews, including her biographer, James-Edward, would also enter the church.) There was also the mysterious young clergyman Jane met at the Devon resort. And there always seem to be plenty of other clergymen turning up in Jane's letters. So that would pretty easily explain why there are so many men from that calling in the novels. But a more interesting and complex question is: How are the clergymen in Jane Austen's novels presented? As is usually the case with Jane Austen, the answer is that they are presented differently in different novels and even within the same novel.

Perhaps the most famous clergyman in Austen's novels is Mr. Collins, the absurd, pompous, obsequious cousin of the Bennets who is in line to inherit Mr. Bennet's property because the Bennets have no sons (although they do have five daughters). Mr. Collins cannot praise his patroness, the formidable Lady Catherine de Bourgh, highly or often enough. He proposes to Elizabeth in the most ludicrous (and hilarious) speech imaginable and, when she refuses him, quickly finds a more willing victim in Elizabeth's friend Charlotte: "Mr. Collins to be sure was neither sensible nor agreeable; his society was irksome, and his attachment to her must be imaginary. But still he would be her husband." The fact that he starts back in horror at the sight of a novel, and protests that he never reads novels, is a pretty severe condemnation in itself. But he also writes a cruel, mean-spirited, stupid letter to Mr. Bennet during the Lydia crisis, showing not a trace of Christian charity. If he were meant to be representative of clergymen, the profession could hardly have done worse.

Mr. Elton, the clergyman Emma tries to match up with her friend Harriet, is not quite so ridiculous but he too has far more negative character traits than positive ones—he is foolish, affected, vain, and, again, cruel. He and his vulgar bride Mrs. Elton conspire to insult and humiliate poor Harriet in public, in just one of *their* uncharitable actions.

More positively, the irresistible Henry Tilney, the charming hero of *Northanger Abbey*, is a clergyman, as is the kind, respectable father of Catherine Morland, that novel's heroine. Edward Ferrars, who marries the heroine Elinor in *Sense and Sensibility*, explains that while he had an inclination for the church, the profession was not fashionable enough in the eyes of his family. He does choose it eventually, however, and stands as another more positive figure of a clergyman—although to many readers he has never seemed forceful enough to be a hero (Hugh Grant notwithstanding!).

In *Mansfield Park*, the clergyman Mr. Grant is criticized by the novel even if his sermons are allowed to be good, but he does not stand alone to represent the clergy in that book. For it is in *Mansfield Park* that Austen directly addresses the subject of the role clergymen play in English society. Mary Crawford echoes the opinion of Edward Ferrars's family when she says to Edmund Bertram, "For what is to be done in the church? Men love to distinguish themselves, and in either of the other lines, distinction may be gained, but not in the church. A clergyman is nothing." Edmund replies that he "cannot call that situation nothing, which has the charge of all that is of the first importance to mankind, individually or collectively considered, temporally and eternally—which has the guardianship of religion and morals, and consequently of the manners which result from their influence." In response to this, and much more that Edmund says in eloquent defense of the church, Mary responds, "You really are fit for something better. Come, do change your mind. It is not too late. Go into the law." And he doesn't see her response as a red flag, but believes she is the woman for him! She argues the subject with him in other places, allowing Austen an extended defense of the church in this novel.

Jane Austen's father and the other clergymen Austen knew best were good men, and she was religious enough herself to place a high value on the role they played in society, both locally and nationally. Although clergymen appear in many places and in many forms in her writing, it is really only in *Mansfield Park*, of all her novels, that the profession itself is discussed, and there Austen praises it most highly.

60 "FINE NAVAL FERVOUR" I: FRANK AUSTEN

Louisa Musgrove in *Persuasion* has "fine naval fervour," and so did her creator. Let's take a look at how this came to be.

Francis Austen, the fifth Austen son, was born in April 1774, which makes him the member of the family closest in age to Jane. We've seen how Jane would later describe his childhood personality—his "insolence of spirit"—in a poem. Though small for his age, "Fly," as Frank was called in the family, was fearless and active. Family tradition says that at the age of seven he bought a pony called Squirrel and later, after riding him for several seasons, sold him for quite a bit more than he had paid. His first suit was made from his mother's scarlet riding habit, which she had worn at her wedding. Frank—Fly—would wear this outfit hunting. We certainly get the image of a lively, resourceful little boy from these accounts of Frank Austen's childhood.

It should perhaps come as no surprise that at the age of twelve he went off to attend naval school at the Royal Academy at Portsmouth. He did well at the Academy, leaving it at the age of fourteen (shockingly young to us!) to sail aboard the *Perseverance* to the East Indies. As was not unusual in those days, he didn't see his family again for five years. While he was gone, Jane dedicated stories to "Francis William Austen Esqr Midshipman on board his Majesty's Ship the Perseverance." Jane was proud to have a brother with such an illustrious title.

Frank moved up the ranks and was a good officer. In both his personal and professional life, he was by all accounts decent, honest, responsible, generous, modest, and well-liked. But patronage was important for advancement too, and Mr. Austen worked behind the scenes writing letters to help his son get promoted. By 1798 Frank had been promoted to commander.

When Mr. Austen died, Jane gave Frank—or held for him—their father's compass and scissors as mementoes. It is notable that at this time, when the brothers were offering to pitch in to help their mother and sisters, Frank immediately offered to contribute £100 per year—twice as much as James and Henry—and asked them to keep this offer a secret. The secret was not kept, however, and Mrs. Austen was moved and gratified by such generosity. She insisted on accepting only half the amount Frank had offered. As we've seen, Mrs. Austen, Jane, Cassandra, and Martha would live with Frank and his new young bride, Mary (who brought no money to the marriage), in Southampton. Frank left a pregnant Mary in the care of his mother and sisters when he went back to sea.

Frank's nephew James-Edward describes how Frank was a strict disciplinarian aboard ship (as was his duty) but also a very religious man: "He was spoken of as '*the* officer who kneeled at church.'" Frank saw a great deal of action in his career and was one of Admiral Nelson's favorite captains, but by a cruel twist of fate he missed the Battle of Trafalgar, to his great disappointment.

Five years after Mary died giving birth to their eleventh child, Frank married Martha Lloyd. He continued to see steady promotion in his old age, and he continued to go to sea. Frank Austen became Sir Francis, Knight Commander of the Bath, and was once again left a widower. At eighty-nine he was made Admiral of the Fleet. Frank Austen died at the age of ninety-one, the longest lived of the eight Austen children. He had lived more than twice as long as his sister Jane, who not only loved him dearly but always held his character and accomplishments in the highest regard.

61 "Fine naval fervour" II: Charles Austen

Charles Austen, the sixth son, born in 1779, was the baby of the family. He followed in the footsteps of his brother Frank, also attending the Royal Academy at Portsmouth. Mr. Austen's letter-writing campaign seems to have worked in his favor too, although Charles did not have the same degree of success as Frank in his naval career.

He had a "sweet temper and affectionate disposition," according to his nephew, which endeared him not only to his family but to all who served under him. He was very close to his sisters, and read Jane's novels with pride and pleasure. One example of his affection for Jane and Cassandra can be seen in his buying them gold chains and topaz crosses with his prize money—that is, money earned from capturing enemy ships. "He must be well scolded," Jane writes to Cassandra, obviously delighted with this sweet display of their brother's love and thoughtfulness. Readers of *Mansfield Park* will recognize Jane's use of this incident in the novel, though she changes some of the details. Fanny Price's sailor brother William will give her an amber cross, which she treasures.

Jane's letters show how anxious the family always was for news of both sailor brothers when they were at sea. Information about ships was sometimes hard to come by. Charles would leave for North America Station in 1804 and not return to England until 1811. He must have missed his close-knit family dearly. He did find other companionship: As we've seen, he married young Fanny Palmer in Bermuda and when he finally returned to England, he brought with him a wife and two small daughters. Fanny would bear Charles another girl before dying giving birth to a fourth, who would also die within weeks. Jane complained that the girls looked too much like their mother's family and not enough like Austens. The eldest girl, Cassy, would live at Chawton Cottage for months at a time after her mother's death.

Charles had more misfortune: His ship was wrecked in the Mediterranean in 1816 and it would be ten years before he would command another one. He struggled with poverty for years. When he did return to sea he was injured in a fall from a mast. He married his dead wife's sister, Harriet, and had four more children, but two of them would die very young.

Charles was eventually promoted to Rear-Admiral. He died of cholera at the age of seventy-three while serving in Burma. The topaz crosses he gave to his beloved big sisters can be seen today at Chawton Cottage. Like his brother Frank, he lives on in the spirit of the sailors in Jane Austen's novels.

62 "Fine naval fervour" III: *Mansfield Park*

We can see where Jane Austen acquired her intimate knowledge of the Royal Navy: from her two sailor brothers, Frank and Charles. How exactly did she use that knowledge in her fiction?

The navy makes important appearances in *Mansfield Park*, in particular regarding two characters: William Price, the spirited young brother of the heroine Fanny, and Admiral Crawford, the uncle of Mary and Henry Crawford. These two naval men could not be more different. "Admiral Crawford," the narrator tells us, "was a man of vicious conduct, who chose, instead of retaining his niece, to bring his mistress under his own roof." Austen gives Mary Crawford a line about her uncle that tells us about both Mary's cynical wit and the behavior of some officers: "Certainly, my home at my uncle's brought me acquainted with a circle of admirals. Of *Rears*, and *Vices*, I saw enough. Now, do not be suspecting me of a pun, I entreat." The degree of vulgarity in Mary's punning here has been the subject of debate among readers, but in any case Fanny and Edmund Bertram are shocked by her open criticism of her uncle.

We know that Mr. Austen wrote letters to influential people in order to help his sons advance in their careers, but in *Mansfield Park* Austen criticizes the tradition of patronage in the navy. Despite the efforts Fanny believes her uncle must be making on William's behalf, the young man is certain he will never be a lieutenant, never get "made." (In *Persuasion*, the point is made that Captain Wentworth was given his first ship—unusually—without the benefit of much influence on his behalf.) Henry Crawford, in order to win Fanny's favor, appeals to his uncle the Admiral to do something for William. This "vicious" man, as a favor to his nephew, is able to use his influence to see that William is promoted to lieutenant at once. The fact that William is a good and worthy sailor, and the heroine's affectionate brother, does not detract from the picture of corruption in the sequence of events as Austen, with harsh irony, exposes the strings pulled at the upper levels of the bureaucracy to effect this promotion.

Still, William Price is himself the picture of decency, and the worldly Henry Crawford is impressed:

> *He longed to have been at sea, and seen and done and suffered as much. . . . The glory of heroism, of usefulness, of exertion, of endurance, made his own habits of selfish indulgence appear in shameful contrast; and he wished he had been a William Price, distinguishing himself and working his way to fortune and consequence with so much self-respect and happy ardour, instead of what he was!*

Of course, Henry's uncle has had too great an influence on his character, and these feelings do not last long.

With Frank's permission, Jane used the names of several of his old ships in this novel. Indeed, Jane Austen was a stickler for accuracy in the details of her writing, and she listened to her brothers talk about their naval experiences very carefully—though no doubt there was much about life at sea, and in action, that these gentlemanly brothers withheld from the ladies of the family. She reproduces the talk of sailors—their jargon and their concerns—with complete credibility, if without the oaths no doubt frequently used, though her brother Frank, at least, never used them himself. Jane's nephew said he thought no flaw had ever been found in Austen's seamanship in either *Mansfield Park* or *Persuasion*. In *Persuasion*, however, we get a different look at the men who chose to be sailors.

63 "FINE NAVAL FERVOUR" IV: *PERSUASION*

Captain Frederick Wentworth, the hero of Austen's last completed novel, *Persuasion*, is a very attractive figure and a very different sort of man from the clergymen (Henry Tilney in *Northanger Abbey*, Edmund Bertram in *Mansfield Park*, and Edward Ferrars in *Sense and Sensibility*) and landowners (Mr. Darcy, Mr. Knightley in *Emma*, and Colonel Brandon in *Sense and Sensibility*) who appeared in earlier novels. Just as portraits of the younger Austen sons Frank and Charles show them with short, dark hair while their elder brothers used hair powder, the sailors Jane Austen portrays in *Persuasion* are a new, modern breed of self-made men who rise in their professions—and in the world—largely on the basis of their actions. Captain Wentworth was "made commander in consequence of the action off St. Domingo"—a battle in which Frank Austen had in fact seen action himself.

Captain Wentworth had no fortune when he first met and courted Anne, but he "was confident that he should soon be rich." As we know, gentlemen outside the navy often had no way to become rich but to marry women with good fortunes. But Captain Wentworth, in the eight years since he met Anne, has taken so many "prizes"—enemy ships—that he has *made himself* a rich man. He is "brilliant," "headstrong," and "full of life and ardour." He has "the frank, the open-hearted, the eager character" Anne so highly values. Add to all this his daring and difficult occupation, and he is without doubt the most romantic of Austen's heroes.

Captain Wentworth and the profession he represents are especially appealing as Austen contrasts them with members of the old order like Anne's father, Sir Walter, for whom social position, wealth, and, in Sir Walter's absurd case, physical appearance, are everything.

Other sailors in *Persuasion*, with the exception of dead Dick Musgrove, are also presented as good men (although the navy does receive some criticism for neglecting the maintenance of its ships). Anne enjoys speaking to Captain Benwick about poetry, and she becomes quite fond of Admiral Croft, who, unlike Frank Austen, "was in the Trafalgar action." Captain Harville is also shown to have an excellent character. In later years modest Frank suspected he might have been the model not for the hero but for Captain Harville, particularly in that character's habits around the house at Lyme: Captain Harville "drew, he varnished, he carpentered, he glued; he made toys for the children, he fashioned new netting-needles and pins with improvements; and if every thing else was done, sat down to his large fishing-net at one corner of the room." It seems Jane got a good look at this aspect of Frank's character—his domestic industriousness—when they shared the house in Southampton.

Anne Elliot greatly admires the men of the Royal Navy and is thrilled to marry one, though Jane Austen knew well the privations, dangers, and loneliness of the naval life. Her heroine, she tells us, "gloried in being a sailor's wife," and Jane Austen clearly gloried in being the sister of two distinguished sailors.

64 So who was the real Mr. Darcy? (And Mr. Knightley, and Captain Wentworth . . .)

There has been much speculation about the identities of possible real-life prototypes for these characters, but for the most part it does not seem that Jane Austen modeled her characters upon specific people she knew. Certainly, there are elements that are recognizable—character traits, occupations, situations—but it appears that Jane's genius was such that she created Emma Woodhouse and Henry Tilney and the rest of the amazing cast of characters in the universe of her novels largely out of her imagination.

As we've seen, there are resemblances to real-life situations—adoptions resembling Edward's recur as part of the story line, and Jane did receive that cross from Charles, which no doubt inspired Fanny's present of a cross from *her* sailor brother. There are also repetitions so insistent you feel they must have some correspondence in Jane's life: for example, the continual reappearance of weak or dead mothers. But particular individuals, if they were used as models, have been distilled into something unrecognizable—at least to us looking back over the distance of two centuries. It is in most cases not apparent who the originals would have been, and we get no help from Austen herself. If they are portraits drawn from life, either she did not write of the fact or those discreet guardians of her private musings left no trace of it.

Jane's nephew wrote that she observed nature and used only what existed *in* nature, but the artist of genius like his aunt creates new combinations of these features "so that they are nature, but not exactly the same nature which had come before his eyes." James-Edward Austen-Leigh goes on to say that no one in the family ever recognized any of her characters as a particular individual and that his aunt disapproved of what she called "such an 'invasion of social proprieties.'" Jane's brother Henry also wrote that she never drew from individuals for her characters, despite speculation to the contrary. Austen-Leigh quite rightly says Jane Austen wanted "to create, not to reproduce." He tells us she claimed to be "'too proud of my gentlemen to admit that they were only Mr. A. or Colonel B.'" When we consider Austen's gentlemen—Mr. Darcy, Mr. Knightley, Captain Wentworth, and all the others—that statement has the ring of truth.

65 BAD BOYS

Jane Austen's novels contain quite a few bad boys, and three in particular have a family resemblance. These three are all attractive, and all three are connected with seduction plots that seem to have come out of a different kind of novel and from a different kind of writer.

In *Pride and Prejudice*, Mr. Wickham completely charms Elizabeth Bennet from the beginning of their acquaintance: "His manners recommended him to every body. Whatever he said, was said well; and whatever he did, done gracefully. Elizabeth went away with her head full of him." Elizabeth, along with everybody else, is mistaken about his character. Mr. Darcy's letter reveals that Wickham, who was living "a life of idleness and dissipation," had persuaded Mr. Darcy's fifteen-year-old sister, Georgiana, to elope with him with the sinister double motive of securing Georgiana's fortune and revenging himself on Mr. Darcy. Later, of course, he will run off with Lydia Bennet with no intention of marrying her.

Before these revelations, Wickham had presented the much more interesting picture of an attractive man who must find a woman whose fortune will support him. Austen shows us how Wickham's charms cloud Elizabeth's judgment in this regard: "Less clear-sighted perhaps in his case than in Charlotte's, [she] did not quarrel with him for his wish of independence." Once she discovers his true character, however, judgment becomes a matter of black and white. Wickham is now an old-fashioned villain and not the complex, morally ambiguous man who would seem to fit better into Jane Austen's realism. Indeed, he is rehabilitated somewhat at the end of the novel by marrying Lydia instead of abandoning her to a life of misery and disgrace.

Similarly, in *Sense and Sensibility*, Willoughby is not simply the faithless lover who breaks Marianne's heart by dumping her in order to marry a rich woman. He too, it is revealed "offstage," has done much worse. As Colonel Brandon tells Elinor, "He had left the girl whose youth and innocence he had seduced, in a situation of the utmost distress, with no creditable home, no help, no friends, ignorant of his address!"

Willoughby later makes a lame excuse for this behavior that does nothing to lessen its evil.

Most interesting of these three charmer-seducers is Henry Crawford in *Mansfield Park*, who does not run off with the married Maria Rushworth until the end of the novel. Until that time, his character seems to be steadily improving, and he—unlike Wickham and Willoughby—charms *the reader* completely. It is therefore hard for most readers to accept that this dazzlingly intelligent, witty, spirited man, who acts so thoughtfully and energetically on Fanny's behalf, should be responsible for Maria's seduction and ruin. To be sure, Maria is not an innocent young girl. Indeed, the extent to which matters go between her and Henry "was the result of her imprudence; and he went off with her at last, because he could not help it." Still, it bothers many readers to see this complex character in this most complex of novels done away at the end of the novel with a seduction plot that is not materially different from those used by Austen in novels she drafted in the eighteenth century.

66 BAD PARENTS

We've seen what good parents Mr. and Mrs. Austen were. So why are there so few good parents—and so many bad ones—in Jane Austen's novels? Let's look at some examples.

Mrs. Bennet, in *Pride and Prejudice*, has spoiled the youngest daughter, Lydia, because she very much mirrors her young self back to her. So Lydia grows up "untamed, unabashed, wild, noisy, and fearless," with no regard for the feelings or welfare of her family. Mr. Bennet, in his own different way, is no better. His response to Elizabeth's articulate, rational plea that he not let Lydia go to Brighton because of the dangers such a place represents to a character like hers is woefully inadequate. Mr. Bennet's irony is still amusing, but it is inappropriate here: "Lydia will never be easy till she has exposed herself in some public place or other, and we can never expect her to do it with so little expense or inconvenience to her family as under the present circumstances." Mr. Bennet fails in his parental duty, and Elizabeth's fears are shown to have been fully justified.

At the end of *Mansfield Park*, Sir Thomas also looks around at the disastrous situation in his family and realizes that he has failed as a father: "He felt that he ought not to have allowed [Maria's] marriage, that his daughter's sentiments had been sufficiently known to him to render him culpable in authorising it, that in so doing he had sacrificed the right to the expedient, and been governed by motives of selfishness and worldly wisdom." And his sanctioning Maria's marriage to the foolish Rushworth is only one part of Sir Thomas's regret: "The anguish arising from the conviction of his own errors in the education of his daughters, was never to be entirely done away." His wife is even worse, mindlessly spending her days on the sofa, completely out of touch with what is happening around her. Lady Bertram is totally unfit to be a mother. Her sister, Fanny Price's natural mother, is a "partial, ill-judging parent, a dawdle, a slattern, who neither taught nor restrained her children," and Fanny's father is also "negligent of his family." What an indictment of parents we find in *Mansfield Park*!

Mr. Woodhouse, Emma's father, has an intellect as weak as Lady Bertram's. Along with that, his anxiety, low spirits, and complete self-absorption make him a bad father, though Emma has been lucky enough to have surrogate parents in the form of Miss Taylor (now Mrs. Weston) and Mr. Knightley, a neighbor whose brother is married to Emma's sister. Although Emma's character certainly suffers from having such a father and no mother (since Mrs. Woodhouse died when Emma was a very little girl), she is lucky that things have not turned out worse.

In *Persuasion*, Anne Elliot also lost her mother early in life and her vain, cold-hearted father has no regard for her at all. Elinor and Marianne Dashwood have lost their father rather than their mother, and though Mrs. Dashwood is a pleasant, loving woman, her excessively romantic and imprudent character causes her to overlook the danger in Marianne's unconventional relationship with Willoughby. Like Elizabeth Bennet, Elinor tries to impress upon her parent that parent's own duty, suggesting that she come right out and ask Marianne whether or not she and Willoughby are engaged. Mrs. Dashwood demurs; Elinor urges her again, "but in vain; common sense, common care, common prudence, were all sunk in Mrs. Dashwood's romantic delicacy." This otherwise good woman is grossly negligent in this affair.

Catherine Morland's parents are not much seen in *Northanger Abbey*, and they seem good enough people, if not very perceptive where their children's hearts are concerned. But Catherine's guardians in Bath are the Allens, and Mrs. Allen is no proper guide at all for young Catherine, who is herself totally ignorant of social rules and desperately in need of instruction.

When Mr. Allen steps in to warn Catherine about the impropriety of young ladies being "frequently driven about in [open carriages] by young men, to whom they are not even related," Catherine exclaims over Mrs. Allen's not having told her this before: "I always hoped you would tell me, if you thought I was doing wrong," she cries. But Mrs. Allen wouldn't know how to instruct Catherine on matters of "'real consequence'" (as opposed to which color gown to wear) if her life depended on it!

It is impossible to miss this pattern in Jane Austen's novels—bad parents and bad guardians are everywhere. It's pretty clear that these figures weren't based on her own parents, but she no doubt witnessed bad parenting in other households, and we can take this as one more instance of her writing not directly from personal experience, but by observing what she saw in nature and transforming it in her imagination into something entirely new.

67 BROTHERS AND SISTERS

If parents are largely shown in a negative light in Jane Austen's novels, brothers and sisters receive more mixed treatment. Penelope Watson, in the fragment called *The Watsons*, has destroyed her sister Elizabeth's prospects for happiness by acting from motives of rivalry to set the man Elizabeth loved against her. Their sister Emma is shocked to hear this: "Could a sister do such a thing?—Rivalry, treachery between sisters!" she exclaims, no doubt voicing Austen's opinion.

In *Mansfield Park*, Maria and Julia Bertram compete quite ruthlessly for the attentions of Henry Crawford. Once Henry's preference for Maria becomes apparent, "[Julia's] heart was sore and angry. . . . The sister with whom she was used to be on easy terms, was now become her greatest enemy; they were alienated from each other, and Julia was not superior to the hope of some distressing end to the attentions which were still carrying on there, some punishment to Maria. . . ." These sisters get along only when their love is not tested in any way, but "the sisters, under such a trial as this, had not affection or principle enough to make them merciful or just, to give them honour or compassion. Maria felt her triumph, and pursued her purpose careless of Julia."

In *Persuasion*, Anne Elliot envies the perfect amity between Louisa and Henrietta Musgrove, which offers such a contrast to what she finds in her own family. Her sisters offer her neither real love—Mary's attachment to her is selfish and superficial—nor understanding.

But on the positive side, Austen presents many happy pictures of sibling devotion. Elizabeth and Jane Bennet share not only each other's confidence, but, despite their very different personalities, intelligence, good sense, and values. The love between them is not simply a matter of their having been born into the same family. Austen frequently shows that that is not always a strong enough bond in itself to ensure a strong mutual attachment. (Mr. Darcy's primary offense, in Elizabeth's view, is the harm he's done to Jane by separating Mr. Bingley from her.) In contrast, Emma Woodhouse and her sister love each other very much, but Emma must be content with that benefit of having a sister, for Isabella cannot "meet her in conversation, rational or playful," any more than Mr. Wood-house can.

The Knightley brothers in *Emma* can hold intelligent conversation, greeting each other without much apparent emotion but "burying under a calmness that seemed all but indifference, the real attachment which would have led either of them, if requisite, to do every thing for the good of the other." No doubt Jane observed this "true English style" in her own household.

In *Northanger Abbey*, the brother and sister of Catherine Morland's friend Isabella Thorpe are rude and inconsiderate to other family members, and John Dashwood in *Sense and Sensibility* is worse than rude: He allows his wife to talk him out of giving his mother and sisters the financial assistance he knows it is his duty to give them. But in this novel we also see the powerful love that exists between those sisters, brought out most movingly when Elinor watches over Marianne in her illness, in which she comes very close to death. The sisters share a stronger bond with each other than with the men they will marry.

In *Mansfield Park*, Edmund Bertram is almost like a brother to Fanny Price, and she falls in love with this brother-like figure, but she seems to have even stronger feelings for her real brother William. Even the morally questionable Crawfords, brother and sister, are devoted to each other. In this novel Austen writes that in some ways "even the conjugal tie is beneath the fraternal. Children of the same family, the same blood, with the same first associations and habits, have some means of enjoyment in their power, which no subsequent connections can supply." It is not surprising to find Jane Austen expressing this opinion. She was devoted to her brothers and sister as they were devoted to her. Certainly, they could hurt and irritate her, and she captures or creates with great skill the varying kinds and degrees of trouble and pain siblings can cause each other. But Austen herself never found any stronger human bonds than those forged in the rectory at Steventon in the early years of her life.

68 HUSBANDS AND WIVES

"Had Elizabeth's opinion been all drawn from her own family, she could not have formed a very pleasing picture of conjugal felicity or domestic comfort." So the narrator of *Pride and Prejudice* says about Elizabeth Bennet. Readers of Jane Austen might say the same thing if they derived their opinions of the married state from the pictures of marriage presented in her novels. Although Austen always leaves her heroines at the beginning of what promises to be a blissful married life, that image of matrimony is decidedly different from almost anything we've seen in the previous chapters. Why should this be so?

Austen returns again and again to the idea that many, if not most, husbands and wives are ill-matched. One major reason for this is that husbands so often pick wives on the basis of their good looks and youthful spirits. This was the case with Mr. Bennet:

Captivated by youth and beauty, and that appearance of good humour, which youth and beauty generally give, [he] had married a woman whose weak understanding and illiberal mind, had very early in their marriage put an end to all real affection for her. Respect, esteem, and confidence, had vanished forever; and all his views of domestic happiness were overthrown.

Sir Thomas Bertram, from *Mansfield Park*, might be described by that passage also, since he too was captivated by youth and beauty when he married Miss Maria Ward and ended up with a wife more interested in her pug than her children. Sir Thomas is an intelligent man, as is Mr. Bennet, and both have wives with whom they cannot hold rational conversations. As Mr. Knightley tells Emma, "Men of sense . . . do not want silly wives."

In *Persuasion* we see the sexes reversed. Anne Elliot's mother was as foolish as Mr. Bennet and Sir Thomas: "Lady Elliot had been an excellent woman, sensible and amiable; whose judgment and conduct, if they might be pardoned the youthful infatuation which made her Lady Elliot, had never required indulgence afterwards." And yet she married Sir Walter, of whose character "vanity was the beginning and the end."

Emma Woodhouse's mother had Emma's intellect and yet she married a man "without activity of mind or body." What woman with a brain could bear to live as the wife of Mr. Woodhouse?

We've seen the mismatch of Fanny Price's Aunt and Uncle Bertram. Her parents chose just as badly. Mrs. Price should have at least married a man with money, since she doesn't have the disposition, talents, or character to bring up a large family on a small income. Mr. Price is dirty and vulgar, coarse and loud, but the fact that he becomes a different man, with manners "more than passable," in response to Henry Crawford shows that he improves with better company than his wife offers. He should have married a woman who would have brought out his better nature.

In these and many other cases we see that Austen believes husbands must choose wives, and wives, husbands, who are suitable; specifically—ideally—who will bring out the best in each other. In each novel we see the unhappy results when individuals marry in consequence of a blind and foolish infatuation with the wrong traits.

69 "Connubial felicity"

There are some exceptions in Austen's novels to the rule that seems to hold there that most marriages are not very good ones. Some of these seemingly good marriages are barely described, and it is rather the absence of unfavorable descriptions and the overall quality of the individuals concerned that allow the reader to infer that the marriages are good. Such is the case with Elizabeth Bennet's aunt and uncle, Mr. and Mrs. Gardiner; the Musgroves in *Persuasion* (the parents of Charles, Louisa, and Henrietta); Mr. and Mrs. Morland in *Northanger Abbey*; and Mr. and Mrs. Weston in *Emma*. But there is one couple in *Persuasion* whose marriage is specifically discussed in positive terms, and that is Admiral and Mrs. Croft. Let's take a look at them.

Mrs. Croft, the sister of Captain Wentworth, is shown to be more discriminating than her husband. Admiral Croft cannot distinguish between Louisa and Henrietta Musgrove, and thinks either one would do as a wife for his brother-in-law: "And very nice young ladies they both are; I hardly know one from the other." His wife appears to think a little differently: "'Very good humoured, unaffected girls, indeed,' said Mrs. Croft, in a tone of calmer praise, such as made Anne suspect that her keener powers might not consider either of them as quite worthy of her brother." Notice how Mrs. Croft does not flatly contradict her husband, as a bad partner would (Mary Musgrove, for example, determined to be right at any cost), even though she has a different opinion. And although Admiral Croft can't tell Louisa from Henrietta, he is not stupid: he has a different kind of intelligence, perfectly suited to his profession. He is a man of action, a sailor.

As Anne rides with the Admiral and his wife in their gig (an offer her snobbish sister Mary has declined, possibly because she "could not endure to make a third in a one horse chaise") she witnesses the way the Crofts interact:

> "My dear admiral, that post!—we shall certainly take that post."
> But by coolly giving the reins a better direction herself, they happily passed the danger; and by once afterwards judiciously putting out her hand, they neither fell into a rut, nor ran foul of a dung-cart; and Anne, with some amusement at their style of driving, which she imagined no bad representation

of the general guidance of their affairs, found herself safely deposited by them at the cottage.

While Admiral and Mrs. Croft are slightly comical figures, and the avoidance of a dung-cart is of course ridiculous, the admiration of their compatibility is sincere. If superior characters like Anne and Captain Wentworth were to have equal compatibility, the picture would be sublime.

This kind of collaboration shows up in Austen's novels as the sign of a good marriage. Also in *Persuasion*, Captain Harville and his wife appear to be in sync as well. After Louisa Musgrove's accident on the Cobb, the Harvilles come upon a scene of panic and confusion: "Shocked as Captain Harville was, he brought senses and nerves that could be instantly useful; and a look between him and his wife decided what was to be done." The two understand each other so well, they can communicate by a look. Moreover, the Harvilles' very modest house in Lyme strikes Anne as "the picture of repose and domestic happiness," and when she leaves it she "thought she left great happiness behind her."

Such descriptions of domestic happiness are so rare in Austen's novels that their appearance in regard to two couples in which both husbands are naval men indicates yet again the author's very high regard for men of that profession. When the Crofts come to Bath:

They brought with them their country habit of being almost always togeth-er. . . . Anne saw them wherever she went. Lady Russell took her out in her carriage almost every morning, and she never failed to think of them, and never failed to see them. Knowing their feelings as she did, it was a most attractive picture of happiness to her.

A most attractive and very rare picture of connubial bliss in Jane Austen's writing!

70 LOVE AT FIRST SIGHT

"No sooner did I first behold him, than I felt that on him the hap-piness or Misery of my future Life must depend." That, again, is Laura from *Love and Freindship*. Elizabeth Bennet isn't quite so ridiculous, but she does fall for Mr. Wickham, the charming bad-boy seducer, the first time she lays eyes on him: "His appearance was greatly in his favour; he had all the best part of beauty, a fine countenance, a good figure, and very pleasing address. The introduction was followed up on his side by a happy readiness of con-versation—a readiness at the same time perfectly correct and unassuming." Later on, when her sister Jane questions the account Wickham has given of Mr. Darcy's behavior toward him, Elizabeth defends it on the most super-ficial of grounds: "There was truth in his looks."

Elizabeth's opinion of Mr. Darcy, however, which she imparts to him after his first proposal to her, is rather different:

"From the very beginning, from the first moment I may almost say, of my acquaintance with you, your manners impressing me with the fullest belief of your arrogance, your conceit, and your selfish disdain of the feelings of others, were such as to form that ground-work of disapprobation, on which succeeding events have built so immoveable a dislike; and I had not known you a month before I felt that you were the last man in the world whom I could ever be prevailed on to marry."

In both cases, of course, Elizabeth's "first impressions" (the original title of *Pride and Prejudice*, remember) are mistaken. It takes months of acquaintance with Mr. Darcy for Elizabeth to realize that he is exactly the man suited for her. In the example of Elizabeth Bennet, Jane Austen explicitly rejects the romantic idea of love at first sight:

If the regard springing from [gratitude and esteem] is unreasonable or unnatural, in comparison of what is so often described as arising on a first interview with its object, and even before two words have been exchanged, nothing can be said in her defence, except that she had given somewhat of a trial to the latter method, in her partiality for Wickham, and that its ill-success might perhaps authorise her to seek the other less interesting mode of attachment.

Elizabeth's interest in Wickham didn't go far enough, or long enough, for her to be much hurt by it, but not every heroine has her instincts for self-preservation.

In *Sense and Sensibility*, Marianne Dashwood similarly falls for Willoughby too quickly, and takes offense when her sister suggests that she doesn't really know him very well: "'You are mistaken, Elinor,' said she warmly, 'in supposing I know very little of Willoughby. I have not known him long indeed, but I am much better acquainted with him, than with any other creature in the world, except yourself and mama.'" Just as in Elizabeth's case, Marianne is shown to be greatly mistaken in her judgment of the man. She is also shown to have been wrong in her initial judgment of Colonel Brandon as old and infirm, and, at thirty-five, past the stage when he could be moved by feelings of romantic love.

Both Marianne and Elizabeth are saved from marrying their first favorites and in that regard are much luckier than the men and women who pick spouses based on superficial criteria without a real knowledge of their characters and live to regret their bad decisions. Which is not to say there aren't some few lucky ones—even in Jane Austen's novels—whose first impressions are correct and do not lead them astray. As Mrs. Croft says regarding her own engagement to the Admiral, "If Miss Elliot were to hear how soon we came to an understanding, she would never be persuaded that we could be happy together."

71 "PICTURES OF PERFECTION"

From her earliest writings, Jane Austen mocked the convention that a novel's heroine had to be perfect. No Bridget Joneses for the eighteenth-century novel-reading crowd! In *Love and Freindship*, the heroine Laura describes herself: "Lovely as I was, the Graces of my Person were the least of my Perfections. Of every accomplishment accustomary to my sex, I was Mistress. . . . In my Mind, every Virtue that could adorn it was centered; it was the Rendezvous of every good Quality and of every noble sentiment." In the "Plan of a Novel" inspired by suggestions from Mr. Clarke, the heroine is a "faultless Character herself." "Perfection" was a condition that could only be made entertaining to Austen by mockery of it, hence the great number of absurdly idealized heroines in the juvenilia. But in a letter to her niece Fanny, Austen states straightforwardly what she shows ironically: "Pictures of perfection as you know make me sick & wicked."

In the same letter Austen mentions that she has another novel ready for publication. That is *Persuasion*, and of the heroine Anne Elliot, she writes, "You may *perhaps* like the Heroine, as she is almost too good for me." Many readers have found the moral perfection of Fanny Price, the heroine of *Mansfield Park*, much more objectionable, at least partly because it is paired with a judgmental and priggish attitude. With the possible complication of the issue in these two cases (and few readers seem to discover the objection to Anne Elliot that Austen raises in the letter), Jane Austen's heroines in the mature novels interest, excite, move, and amuse us with all their imperfections in ways that "pictures of perfection" never could.

72 EMMA WOODHOUSE

According to her nephew, Jane Austen was "very fond of Emma, but did not reckon on her being a general favourite; for, when commencing that work, she said, 'I am going to take a heroine whom no one but myself will much like.'" The generally accepted view is that *Emma* is the greatest of Austen's novels: the most brilliant, the most technically accomplished, the most polished—in fact, just about perfect. If the novel is perfect, however, the novel's heroine is very far from a "picture of perfection," despite the fact that, as the opening line has it, "Emma Woodhouse, handsome, clever, and rich, with a comfortable home and happy disposition, seemed to unite some of the best blessings of existence; and had lived nearly twenty-one years in the world with very little to distress or vex her." What could Emma be lacking? As is usually the case in Austen's novels, this heroine has to come to understand the world and in particular herself, for with all her cleverness she is, as the movie loosely based upon this book has it, *Clueless*.

Mr. Knightley, very early on, describes Emma's faults to Mrs. Weston: "She will never submit to any thing requiring industry and patience, and a subjection of the fancy to the understanding." And yet, this powerful "fancy" is a large part of Emma's appeal. Emma's intelligence has few outlets, so it works overtime to provide her with interesting stories with little basis in the real world of facts. Mr. Knightley adds that Emma is "spoiled by being the cleverest of her family. . . . She was always quick and assured." Mr. Knightley points out the drawbacks in what we would normally think of as positive attributes—intelligence, confidence—and he does not connect all this with what he says next, but we should: "There is an anxiety, a curiosity in what one feels for Emma. I wonder what will become of her!" Of course, he is in love with her, but the combination of Emma's attractions and her flaws is irresistible.

One of Mr. Knightley's concerns about Emma's relationship with Harriet Smith is that Emma will not think she "'has any thing to learn herself, while Harriet is presenting such a delightful inferiority.'" The friendship is hindering the education he knows she needs. Emma cannot continue to give free rein to her dangerous imagination and cruel wit, and her great energy must be properly channeled, but without that imagination and wit and energy her story would not have its unmatched power to fascinate readers. Emma praises tenderness of heart: "There is nothing to be compared to it. Warmth and tenderness of heart, with an affectionate, open manner, will beat all the clearness of head in the world, for attraction." Indeed, her own heart *is* too hard. But when on another occasion she follows up her resolution to emulate Harriet's "simplicity and modesty" with the point that "It was rather too late in the day to set about being simpleminded and ignorant," we can only laugh and be thankful. Let Emma improve her character after the novel has ended. As readers, we must agree with Mr. Knightley, who knows Emma's bad points better than anyone, when he finds her "faultless in spite of all her faults."

73 "ALL YOUNG LADIES ACCOMPLISHED!"

Early in *Pride and Prejudice*, when Elizabeth Bennet is staying at Netherfield in order to attend her sick sister Jane, she takes part in a discussion of "accomplished women." Mr. Darcy says he doesn't know more than six who are "really accomplished," and Miss Bingley agrees that she doesn't either:

> *"Then," observed Elizabeth, "you must comprehend a great deal in your idea of an accomplished woman."*
>
> *"Yes; I do comprehend a great deal in it."*
>
> *"Oh! certainly," cried his faithful assistant, "no one can be really esteemed accomplished, who does not greatly surpass what is usually met with. A woman must have a thorough knowledge of music, singing, drawing, dancing, and the modern languages, to deserve the word; and besides all this, she must possess a certain something in her air and manner of walking, the tone of her voice, her address and expressions, or the word will be but half deserved."*
>
> *"All this she must possess," added Darcy, "and to all this she must yet add something more substantial, in the improvement of her mind by extensive reading."*

Mr. Darcy and Miss Bingley seem to be getting their ideas of accomplished women not from real life but from literature. The paragons they describe can be found in abundance in the eighteenth-century novels Jane Austen read—and then satirized in so much of her early fiction. In this scene Elizabeth Bennet voices her creator's skepticism about the existence of such women in life as well as in fiction: "I am no longer surprised at your knowing *only* six accomplished women. I rather wonder now at your knowing *any*. . . . *I* never saw such a woman. *I* never saw such capacity, and taste, and application, and elegance, as you describe, united." Once Austen goes from mocking the ideal of a heroine to creating realistic ones, she no longer endows her heroines with superhuman talents.

As we've seen, Elizabeth Bennet and Emma Woodhouse are only middling musical performers. While the extraordinary talents of wonderfully gifted heroines like Laura from *Love and Freindship* need no rational explanation—natural genius alone could account for the way such heroines quickly and inevitably surpass their instructors in every subject—Austen's realistic portrayals contain such explanations. In *Pride and Prejudice*, Elizabeth, sitting at the piano, says, "My fingers . . . do not move over this instrument in the masterly manner which I see so many women's do. They have not the same force or rapidity, and do not produce the same expression. But then I have always supposed it to be my own fault—because I would not take the trouble of practicing." How prosaically unheroic, to require practice in order to excel!

Emma Woodhouse also knows that while some amount of the difference between her playing and singing and Jane Fairfax's might be the result of Jane's natural talent, most of her musical inferiority can readily be explained by "the idleness of her childhood"—she did not practice. And Emma fails to excel in another of Miss Bingley's requirements, drawing, because, again, "steadiness had always been wanting." As Mr. Knightley said, "She will never submit to any thing requiring industry and patience . . . ," and every item on the list of accomplishments requires those.

Catherine Morland, the heroine of *Northanger Abbey*, whom Austen describes in relentlessly "anti-heroic" terms, overshoots this middle ground of accomplishment and goes all the way to the unaccomplished extreme. She could not bear taking piano lessons and gave them up after one year, and "she had no notion of drawing." She also shirked her French lessons. It's unfortunate that with such propensities, like almost all real women, and like almost no literary heroines before her, she "never could learn or understand any thing before she was taught; and sometimes not even then. . . ."

Jane Austen herself was what we would certainly consider accomplished, although she was too modest about her singing and playing to consider herself so. Her brother Henry said she also drew well. She knew French and at least some Italian. She certainly fulfilled Mr. Darcy's requirement that a woman improve her mind "by extensive reading." And there seems to be one accomplishment that Jane Austen's heroines found the time to excel in, and in that they mirror their creator—and that, of course, is dancing.

74 "RATHER NATURAL THAN HEROIC"

Catherine Morland, the heroine of *Northanger Abbey*, is a great fan of Gothic novels but somehow, although she has been "in training for a heroine" since the age of fifteen, she has failed to absorb the "rules" for heroic behavior contained in her favorite books. Until Catherine reaches Northanger Abbey itself, her responses are decidedly those of a normal girl.

As we have seen, Catherine has not reached the extraordinary level of accomplishment befitting a heroine. In fact, her whole family is unheroic. When she sets off for a six-week stay in Bath with family friends, her parents also do not behave like characters in books:

> *Every thing indeed relative to this important journey was done, on the part of the Morlands, with a degree of moderation and composure, which seemed rather consistent with the common feelings of common life, than with the refined susceptibilities, the tender emotions which the first separation of a heroine from her family ought always to excite.*

The Morlands seem to be justified in their lack of concern, at least for the first part of Catherine's trip, for nothing seriously alarming occurs on the journey to Bath (no robbers, tempests, or overturns, as would be seen in a novel), and once there the only threat to Catherine is that she won't ever have a dancing partner.

Once Catherine meets Henry Tilney, she has more opportunity to demonstrate the technique she should have absorbed from the heroines of novels, but Austen has other ideas. After Catherine makes the acquaintance of the charming Mr. Tilney, he seems to disappear from Bath. He reappears with a pretty young woman on his arm,

whom Catherine immediately guessed to be his sister; thus unthinkingly
throwing away a fair opportunity of considering him lost to her forever,
by being married already. But guided only by what was simple and prob-
able, it had never entered her head that Mr. Tilney could be married. . . .
[T]herefore, instead of turning a deathlike paleness, and falling in a fit on
Mrs. Allen's bosom, Catherine sat erect, in the perfect use of her senses,
and with cheeks only a little redder than usual.

Catherine is guided by the simple and probable in all her dealings with Henry Tilney in Bath, whereas the heroines of sentimental and Gothic novels are never so guided. But then they never meet other people, or experience events, that are simple and probable either!

After an unsatisfactory night at a dance, Catherine's unhappiness "took the direction of extraordinary hunger." So she eats and then feels very tired and goes to bed: "She immediately fell into a sound sleep which lasted nine hours, and from which she awoke perfectly revived, in excellent spirits, with fresh hopes and fresh schemes." A proper heroine does not have a good appetite when she is unhappy! And as for sleeping soundly—well, as we've seen, Marianne in *Sense and Sensibility* has given us a much better model for a heroine: "Marianne would have thought herself very inexcusable had she been able to sleep at all the first night after parting from Willoughby." Of course, Marianne is heartbroken and Catherine is only mildly dissatisfied, but part of the joke is that heroines of sensibility are deeply affected by everything—there is no such thing as moderation.

Catherine also fails to keep her heroic dignity in mind at all times. When she speaks to Henry's sister Eleanor she naively and unknowingly reveals her interest in the gentleman. With similar artlessness, she assures Henry himself that she does "'not *want* to talk to any body [else]." Not exactly the formula for stirring in a hero the tormenting pangs of jealousy!

When Catherine sees Henry at the theater after she has unintentionally stood him and his sister up for a planned walk, "Feelings rather natural than heroic possessed her." She "was only eager for an opportunity of explaining" things, and does not take offense at his evident assumption of her guilt in the matter. At the first opportunity, she has no hesitation in blurting out that she has been "quite wild" to apologize and "had ten thousand times rather have been with you." She assures him she would have jumped out of the carriage and run after them if she could have. Henry responds to Catherine's artlessness in an unheroic way himself—he finds it irresistible. When Catherine is later almost tricked into breaking another date with the Tilneys, she goes even further, running to their lodgings, hurrying past the servant at the door, and bursting into the first room she comes to, all in her eagerness to set things right.

The "common feelings of common life" are shown to be much more attractive—and far more entertaining—than the artificial, exaggerated behavior of the literary heroine.

75 PRUDENCE AND ROMANCE

Sense and Sensibility is unique among Austen's novels in having two heroines. Their differences demonstrate two very different ways of living, although, as we've noted, both girls possess sense *and* sensibility—these attributes just have different degrees of influence on their behavior. Marianne, the younger sister, has opinions that are "'all romantic.'" Her sister Elinor remarks that "A few years however will settle her opinions on the reasonable basis of common sense and observation." So, a distinction is clearly drawn between romantic and sensible opinions. In this novel, for the most part, Elinor's sensible and prudent way of operating is shown to be preferable for a number of reasons.

Marianne falls in love with Willoughby pretty much at first sight and assumes because he shares her taste and returns her affection they will be married, despite there not having been any discussion of an engagement. Her equally romantic mother makes the same assumption: "Has not his behaviour to Marianne and to all of us, for at least the last fortnight, declared that he loved and considered her as his future wife?" Elinor, because she usually (but not always) does base her opinions on "common sense and observation," is disturbed. Things do not look right to her. Her mother doesn't have the same concerns because she excuses and rationalizes away any disturbing observations that might interfere with her wishes.

Marianne is just like her mother in this way. When she writes to Willoughby after arriving in London, and he does not reply, she takes comfort in the useful fantasy that the good weather must be keeping sportsmen like him in the country. When he snubs her at a party and then sends her an "impudently cruel" letter, "a letter of which every line was an insult, and which proclaimed its writer to be deep in hardened villany," she persists in imagining that someone else must be responsible for his complete disregard for her feelings and, indeed, the commonest of courtesy: "I could rather believe every creature of my acquaintance leagued together to ruin me in his opinion, than believe his nature capable of such cruelty." She will distort reality with suppositions so unlikely as to be almost impossible before she will give up her cherished visions of the truth.

We are told at the beginning of the novel that Marianne is "everything but prudent." Elinor, on the other hand, has "a strength of understanding, and coolness of judgment, which . . . enabled her frequently to counteract, to the advantage of them all, that eagerness of mind in Mrs. Dashwood which must generally have led to imprudence. . . . [H]er feelings were strong; but she knew how to govern them." Elinor's prudence is seen in action right away, when she must keep Mrs. Dashwood from taking any house that is "too large for their income," as her mother would otherwise do. Later on, she will have to dissuade Marianne from accepting the gift of a horse from Willoughby because the Dashwoods cannot afford to keep a horse. It isn't easy for Marianne to accept the fact and let go of her dream in this case either.

We see Elinor's sense in her prudent decisions concerning money. In matters of love, her good sense is not shown in an inability to feel strongly or to love deeply, but in an ability to keep those feelings under control and not be at their mercy as her sister is. Elinor doesn't nourish her sorrow over what she believes is a hopeless love for Edward Ferrars the way Marianne nourishes hers. Marianne indulges in her misery without any desire to control her emotions. Whereas Marianne seeks "silence, solitude and idleness" as a way to increase her sorrow, Elinor keeps busy, and involved in the concerns of her mother and sisters, so that she might at least hide her sorrow from them.

Marianne's excessive sensibility brings her to the brink of death. As she admits near the end of the novel, had she died, "it would have been self-destruction." She sees and repents all her errors and discovers "the falsehood of her own opinions." Although aspects of Marianne's character are made most attractive, she is chastised for indulging her passions without consideration of the effects her actions have on those who love her. In this novel, Elinor's sense and prudence, combined as they are with strong affections and ready wit (and of course an attractive face and figure), triumph over Marianne's romanticism.

76 GIRLFRIENDS

Jane Austen had quite a few good female friends. We've seen how close she was to Martha Lloyd, Mrs. Lefroy, and the Bigg sisters, whose brother proposed to Jane. Her brother Edward's adoptive mother, Mrs. Knight, also became a close friend. Her cousins Jane and Eliza were her friends too. Outside the family and the neighborhood, she found a good friend in Anne Sharp, the clever governess at Godmersham, and Madame Bigeon and Madame Perigord, of Henry and Eliza's household. Austen knew the value of a good friend, and we can perhaps deduce that she used the same criteria in choosing her companions that Anne Elliot spoke of in *Persuasion*: "My idea of good company, Mr. Elliot, is the company of clever, well-informed people, who have a great deal of conversation." But when we turn to the novels we find few examples of good friendships between women.

The most striking friendship in *Northanger Abbey* is not the good one between Catherine Morland and Henry Tilney's sister, Eleanor, but rather the one between Catherine and the false Isabella Thorpe. Austen's illustrations—by means of Isabella's behavior—of what girlfriends should *not* do are more memorable than the smooth waters of true amity. Isabella is dishonest with Catherine; she uses her again and again (and sometimes tries but fails to do so); she encourages Catherine's interest in Henry Tilney without concern that it might lead to disappointment; she breaks promises to Catherine and calculatingly hurts her feelings; she clearly doesn't "get" Catherine, accusing the most artless person in the world of affectation; and she tries, from selfish motives, to persuade Catherine to do something she thinks is wrong. The whole intimacy between the two girls is premature in the first place since they hardly know each other, and Catherine fairly quickly recovers from the demise of the friendship.

A more interesting and serious case of a vexed friendship is that between Elizabeth Bennet and Charlotte Lucas, "a sensible, intelligent young woman" who is Elizabeth's "intimate friend." Charlotte's speech allows us to see for ourselves that she is quick and amiable, and very compatible with the novel's heroine. However, Charlotte's acceptance of the odious Mr. Collins as a husband persuades Elizabeth that "no real confidence could ever subsist between them again." She is quite sure, as she tells her sister Jane, "that the woman who marries him, cannot have a proper way of thinking." While Elizabeth does visit Charlotte after her wedding, and the novel shows Charlotte's reasons for making a decision Elizabeth finds shocking, Elizabeth's opinion of her friend is never fully restored.

In *Persuasion*, Anne Elliot's one true friend, Lady Russell, does nothing more important than give Anne one piece of what turns out to have been very bad advice. (Her other friend, the invalid Mrs. Smith, praises William Elliot and recommends him to Anne as a husband when she knows he is treacherous and cruel, so she does not much count as a friend.) The most significant friendship in *Emma* is not the heroine's close, warm relationship with the too-indulgent Mrs. Weston, but her disastrous—and brilliantly drawn—"friendship" with Harriet Smith. "You have been no friend to Harriet Smith," Mr. Knightley tells Emma. In this novel we see the most entertaining bad friendship ever imagined.

In Austen's novels, the best friendships are between sisters. Elizabeth Bennet's "disappointment in Charlotte made her turn with fonder regard to her sister, of whose rectitude and delicacy she was sure her opinion could never be shaken." Elizabeth's other true friend is her aunt, Mrs. Gardiner—another close relative. In *Sense and Sensibility*, the sisters Elinor and Marianne have only each other (and their mother) for compatible female companionship.

Although Jane Austen herself had good friends, good friendships are certainly scarce in her novels—but the bad ones are so much fun to read about!

77 "Till this moment, I never knew myself"

Those are the words of Elizabeth Bennet. She has just read Mr. Darcy's letter, written by him after she turned down his proposal of marriage in the strongest possible language, accusing him of ruining her sister Jane's happiness by keeping Mr. Bingley away from her. She also repeated to him Mr. Wickham's long list of Darcy's offenses, expressing her own outrage at them. Up until this point in the novel, Elizabeth has been absolutely certain of all her judgments. When Jane had expressed uncertainty earlier about what to think of Wickham's claims, Elizabeth had replied, "I beg your pardon;— one knows exactly what to think." But now that Mr. Darcy's letter has explained things from his point of view, Elizabeth is forced to reconsider, and then to recognize that her judgments were wrong.

Elizabeth begins reading with "a strong prejudice against every thing he might say" and resists Darcy's version of the truth right down the line, but she is forced, upon replaying past events and conversations, to say to herself, "How differently did every thing now appear. . . ." She realizes that she has been "blind, partial, prejudiced, absurd." In order to come to the conclusions that suited her, she has "'courted prepossession and ignorance, and driven reason away.'" This moment of insight, of self-recognition, is one Elizabeth shares with several of Austen's other heroines, and it is an important moment in the novels.

In *Northanger Abbey*, Catherine Morland's self-knowledge comes after she reveals to Henry Tilney her shocking and absurd suspicion that General Tilney—his father—has murdered his wife—Henry's mother. Henry urges Catherine, "Consult your own understanding, your own sense of the probable, your own observation of what is passing around you." When Catherine does this, she realizes, as did Elizabeth, how she has misjudged matters: "The visions of romance were over. Catherine was completely awakened. . . . [N]othing could shortly be clearer, than that it had been all a voluntary, self-created delusion. . . ." Catherine will soon have other troubles to face, but they won't be preposterous ones created in her imagination.

Emma Woodhouse is the queen of self-created delusions, and we see the trouble they cause her and many around her. One such delusion is that she is in love with Frank Churchill. Even after that little fantasy has faded away, she still has no knowledge of her own heart. She is unaware, until Harriet reveals her own love for Mr. Knightley, how she herself really feels about him, and then: "A few minutes were sufficient for making her acquainted with her own heart. . . . It darted through her, with the speed of an arrow, that Mr. Knightley must marry no one but herself! . . . Her own conduct, as well as her own heart, was before her in the same few minutes. She saw it all with a clearness which had never blessed her before." In the next lines we hear the resemblance to the thoughts of her sister heroine

Elizabeth, although the exact nature of the failings is somewhat different: "How inconsiderate, how indelicate, how irrational, how unfeeling had been her conduct! What blindness, what madness, had led her on!"

Before these heroines can attain their very happy endings, they must open their eyes and see clearly their own hearts, their own conduct, and what has in fact been passing around them. But the delusions are certainly fun for the reader while they last!

78 HOME

We know that Jane Austen was distressed when she was forced to leave her childhood home at Steventon and move to Bath. The idea of home—its loss and its discovery—is important in several of Austen's novels and to several of her heroines in particular. In *Sense and Sensibility*, when the Dashwoods must leave the estate at Norland, the whole family grieves deeply but, as usual, Marianne is more dramatic than Elinor in displaying her emotion: "'Dear, dear Norland!' said Marianne, as she wandered alone before the house, on the last evening of their being there; 'when shall I cease to regret you!—when learn to feel a home elsewhere!'" When Edward Ferrars visits the Dashwoods in their new home at Barton Cottage, she will eagerly ask him how "dear, dear Norland" looks. Austen's romantic heroines—of which Marianne is one—are shown to be especially attached to places that hold early memories.

In *Persuasion*, when the decision is made by the Elliots to rent out Kellynch Hall and find a more modest and economical house for themselves, Anne would prefer to stay in the neighborhood, "where they might . . . still have the pleasure of sometimes seeing the lawns and groves of Kellynch." Of course Anne's wishes are ignored and the new home will be in Bath, so she is suffering from the double evil of "dreading the possible heats of September in all the white glare of Bath, and grieving to forego all the influence so sweet and so sad of the autumnal months in the country." Although Anne is not present when the Crofts take residence, when the day comes, her "heart must be in Kellynch again. A beloved home made over to others; all the precious rooms and furniture, groves, and prospects, beginning to own other eyes and other limbs!" We can see how deeply this loss affects Anne. She is even more strongly attached to the past than Marianne.

Fanny Price, the heroine of *Mansfield Park*, is the one for whom this idea of home will be most important, and she will not simply be faced with the prospect of losing and grieving a beloved home, but of discovering what "home" means. Fanny was taken from her family in Portsmouth at the age of ten and brought to live with her rich aunt and uncle—a small, timid, ashamed, and altogether miserable little girl. When her uncle, for the first time since Fanny came to Mansfield, offers to send her home for a visit to her family in Portsmouth, she is in raptures at the thought, for she still remembers the anguish of that initial wrenching away from them: "It seemed as if to be at home again, would heal every pain that had since grown out of the separation." But to her shock and to the disappointment of all her expectations, she finds that she has been completely mistaken. Her parents show her no love or regard, their house is dirty and unbearably noisy, and soon "she could think of nothing but Mansfield, its beloved inmates, its happy ways. . . . The elegance, propriety, regularity, harmony—and perhaps, above all, the peace and tranquility of Mansfield, were brought to her remembrance every hour of the day, by the prevalence of every thing opposite to them *here*."

Fanny is also appalled by Portsmouth itself: "Sun-shine appeared to her a totally different thing in a town and in the country. Here, its power was only a glare, a stifling, sickly glare, serving but to bring forward stains and dirt that might otherwise have slept." How could a place like that be "home"? The beauty of nature at Mansfield is part of Fanny's attachment to the place. When she receives the summons to return there, her joy and excitement mount. She cannot contain them even though everyone *else* is now miserable. When Edmund takes her back at last, she enters the Park and sees the signs of returning spring with deep pleasure. This is where she belongs.

"When she had been coming to Portsmouth, she had loved to call it her home, had been fond of saying that she was going home; the word had been very dear to her; and so it still was, but it must be applied to Mansfield. *That* was now the home. Portsmouth was Portsmouth; Mansfield was home." This is the knowledge about herself that Fanny—who, unlike Emma or Elizabeth or Catherine, has not been otherwise blind or deluded—must acquire.

79 "She learned romance as she grew older"

"She" is Anne Elliot, the heroine of Austen's last completed novel, *Persuasion*. Here is the whole sentence: "She had been forced into prudence in her youth, she learned romance as she grew older—the natural sequel of an unnatural beginning." We've seen how Austen made fun of romance in much of her earlier writing. Catherine Morland has to reach the point at which "the visions of romance were over"; and Marianne Dashwood, whose "opinions are all romantic," has to learn, through the severest of lessons, that all those romantic opinions of hers are mistaken. And yet, Austen's final novel contains the most romantic story of them all. Jane's sister wrote in her copy of *Persuasion*, in the margin beside the line quoted above: "Dear, dear Jane! This deserves to be written in letters of gold." Did Austen herself learn romance as she grew older?

Almost eight years earlier, Anne and Captain Wentworth had been deeply in love. She had been persuaded to give him up because he had no money. That was certainly the prudent choice, and we've seen in other novels that Austen championed common sense over the false romantic notion that a couple could "exist on Love." But Captain Wentworth was himself convinced that he would be able to *make* his fortune. Anne was convinced also, but let herself be persuaded that the engagement was wrong. As for Captain Wentworth, "All his confidence had been justified. His genius and ardour had seemed to foresee and to command his prosperous path." He did become rich. His expectations might have seemed overly romantic, and in other novels romantic expectations are usually not justified because they are not based on any objective foundation. But this novel shows an individual whose romantic passion itself *commands* his success. Romance is not just a fantasy after all.

Another romantic notion, that of a man or woman carrying a torch for someone for many years, is also dismissed in Austen's other novels, where affections, in due course, are transferred from an old love to a new. Edmund Bertram soon enough finds himself getting over Mary Crawford and falling in love with Fanny Price. Marianne gives up Willoughby and, we are assured, becomes as devoted to Colonel Brandon as she was to the man who broke her heart. Lady Susan's lover, with his "lasting" affections, takes much longer than usual to switch his allegiance to her daughter—one year. But Anne Elliot clings to a hopeless, lost love for *eight* years, and Captain Wentworth never loses his feelings for her either. They are reunited by chance and this time do not let the opportunity slip through their fingers.

The twenty-seven-year-old Anne, who has almost lost the hope of ever marrying, whose story begins in such sadness, has the happiest and most romantic of endings: "More exquisitely happy, perhaps, in their reunion, than when it had been first projected; more tender, more tried, more fixed in a knowledge of each other's character, truth, and attachment. . . ." It seems that visions of romance are not always delusions in Jane Austen's novels.

80 CITY GIRL

Many readers of *Mansfield Park* prefer Mary Crawford to the novel's heroine, Fanny Price. Mary is pretty, accomplished, witty, high-spirited, and sophisticated, whereas Fanny is quiet, sickly, usually low-spirited, and priggish. In being lively and witty, Mary is certainly closer to Elizabeth Bennet and Emma Woodhouse than Fanny is, but does that alone make her a heroine? Whether or not Austen deliberately created a rival heroine in Mary Crawford, she certainly created a most fascinating character.

Mary comes to Mansfield "'with the true London maxim, that every thing is to be got with money,'" and is surprised to find that what holds true in the city is not necessarily true in the country. Mary's wit, as in the amusing anecdote she tells about her inability to locate her harp or hire a cart in which to convey it to her during the harvest, is frequently tinged with cynicism, and sometimes more than tinged. Her opinion of marriage is that "there is not one in a hundred of either sex, who is not taken in when they marry." (We might ask whether Austen's novels don't back Mary up on this!) She disparages her uncle, Admiral Crawford, and the navy in general, in harsh (if witty) terms, much to Fanny and Edmund's disapproval. And her opinion of clergymen is low indeed; she believes only men who are lazy and without ambition go into the church: "A clergyman has nothing to do but to be slovenly and selfish," she says.

In addition to Mary's very quick wit, she has a restless energy that is also attractive. She takes to horseback riding at once: "Miss Crawford's enjoyment of riding was such, that she did not know how to leave off.

Active and fearless, and, though rather small, strongly made, she seemed formed for a horsewoman." She also plays the harp winningly. Fanny, in contrast, does not play at all, and has very low energy: She quickly tires from any physical exertion, whereas Mary must jump up from a bench after sitting for a short time; "'I must move,' said she, 'resting fatigues me.'"

Mary is full of energy, like the city she comes from. Unlike Fanny, "she saw nature, inanimate nature, with little observation." Her great social skills are wonderfully seductive, and the reader, like Edmund Bertram, cannot help being dazzled by her charms. But we should not overlook her serious flaws. As Edmund says, "We do not look in great cities for our best morality," and Mary is a city girl. In addition to Mary's hardness and cynicism, we see that she can be heartless. She has no compassion for Maria and Julia Bertram when her brother Henry is trifling with them both at the same time: "'I rather wonder Julia is not in love with Henry,'" Mary's sister Mrs. Grant observes to her. "'I dare say she is,' replied Mary, coldly. 'I imagine both sisters are.'" When Henry tells Mary he wants to make Fanny fall in love with him while he has no serious intentions toward her, she similarly "left Fanny to her fate." Later, after Mary has tricked Fanny into accepting a necklace Henry actually bought, Fanny thinks how "Miss Crawford . . . was careless as a woman and a friend."

Again and again, we come back to London: "Fanny was disposed to think the influence of London very much at war with all respectable attachments." Mary is ultimately shown to be mercenary and ambitious.

While Edmund is destined to be a mere clergyman she cannot convince herself to marry him, though she has strong feelings for him, but once she thinks his older brother will die and he will inherit Mansfield, she is willing to overlook his profession. As Fanny sees it, "She had only learnt to think nothing of consequence but money." Edmund will see yet a different fault in Mary at the end of the novel: the corrupted principles that account for her cool response to her brother's immoral behavior with Maria Bertram. "This is what the world does," says Edmund, lamenting that Mary Crawford, who had been given so much by nature, should have been "spoilt." Still, even if we know how things end for Mary Crawford in *Mansfield Park*, she seduces us all over again every time we read the book.

81 OBSESSION

One thing that, for all their differences, Jane Austen's heroes and heroines have in common is that their speech ranges over a variety of subjects and can easily adapt to particular situations and company. (Catherine Morland is a partial exception, but we know that with a few more years—and with the influence of Henry Tilney—she will fully join their ranks.) In contrast to these intelligent, flexible speakers, of whom there are of course others in each novel in addition to the hero and heroine, Austen populates her stories with people who turn every conversation back to one subject for wonderful comic effects.

As we've seen, Mrs. Allen, in *Northanger Abbey*, will speak of clothing no matter what the other characters are speaking of. She spends her time in Bath "by the side of Mrs. Thorpe, in what they called conversation, but in which there was scarcely ever any exchange of opinion, and not often any resemblance of subject, for Mrs. Thorpe talked chiefly of her children, and Mrs. Allen of her gowns." In the same novel, boorish John Thorpe speaks of little besides his horse and carriage, boring and frustrating Catherine, since she knows nothing about either subject and cannot even simply listen to him with interest or pleasure. Thorpe is never amusing. His talk is all "idle assertions and impudent falsehoods," and he asserts at one moment what he contradicts the next.

In *Sense and Sensibility*, Sir John Middleton and his wife share a "total want of talent and taste which confined their employments . . . within a very narrow compass. Sir John was a sportsman, Lady Middleton a mother. He hunted and shot, and she humoured her children; and these were their only resources." This narrow-mindedness is a serious character flaw. Sir John is good-natured and generous but he is so limited that when Marianne eagerly inquires of him, "And what sort of a young man is [Willoughby]?" Sir John's amusing but totally inadequate response is, "As good a kind of fellow as ever lived, I assure you. A very decent shot, and there is not a bolder rider in England." The first statement is of course completely untrue. We can trust Sir John's judgment only when he speaks of sports. Marianne presses further, asking about Willoughby's "pursuits, his talents and genius" and Sir John, puzzled, can only say Willoughby is a "pleasant, good humoured fellow, and has got the nicest little black bitch of a pointer

I ever saw." His talk, which reflects his thought, is imprisoned within the confines of his single area of interest.

Mr. Collins, in *Pride and Prejudice*, is almost incapable of speaking in any situation without mentioning his patroness, Lady Catherine de Bourgh. In *Emma*, Mrs. Elton brags incessantly of her brother-in-law's house, Maple Grove, and his two carriages, including the wondrous barouche-landau. Emma's father speaks of health concerns, quite mindlessly, almost every time he opens his mouth, with some variation involving his other absurd hobby-horses—for example, all those "poor" married people who now live with excellent spouses and in truth couldn't be more content.

In *Persuasion*, Charles Musgrove is a sympathetic character, but his limitations save Anne from any regrets for having turned down his offer of marriage, though she likes him as a friend and brother. His lack of conversational ability is a severe defect. Since "he did nothing with much zeal, but sport" he has not much interest in speaking of other subjects. Although he does so sensibly enough sometimes, he is not up to the standard for a hero. It is a lovely stroke that his obsession with sports gives Anne and Captain Wentworth the opportunity to speak to each other alone. Sacrificing an appointment with a gunsmith, good-natured Charles is escorting Anne to her residence in Bath when Captain Wentworth joins them. Charles eagerly asks him,

> *"Are you going near Camden-place? Because if you are, I shall have no scruple in asking you to take my place, and give Anne your arm to her*

father's door. . . . I ought to be at that fellow's in the market-place. He promised me the sight of a capital gun he is just going to send off; said he would keep it unpacked to the last possible moment, that I might see it. . . . By his description, a good deal like the second-sized double-barrel of mine, which you shot with one day, round Winthrop."

You can hear the urgency in his voice. This gun is to him as important as her gown is to Mrs. Allen. In this exquisitely suspenseful moment of the novel, when the emotions of the hero and heroine are at the highest pitch, here is single-minded Charles, completely unaware of their feelings, going on and on about a gun! It is priceless. This disconnect between obsessed speaker and his listeners is one of the brilliant devices by which Jane Austen creates great characters and great comedy.

82 FASHION

As we have seen, Austen herself didn't have much interest in fashion. But did she pass her attitude on to her heroines? On the eve of the cotillion ball, Catherine Morland, the heroine of *Northanger Abbey*, certainly isn't indifferent to clothing: "What gown and what head-dress she should wear on the occasion became her chief concern. . . . she lay awake ten minutes on Wednesday night debating between her spotted and her tamboured muslin, and nothing but the shortness of the time prevented her buying a new one for the evening." But Catherine is only seventeen, and her interest in clothing is of the normal rather than the obsessive variety. The narrator gently chides Catherine for this concern on the grounds that neither men nor other women will admire or like her more for costly attire. "Woman," she says, "is fine for her own satisfaction alone."

Catherine's guardian Mrs. Allen, on the other hand, thinks and speaks of nothing else and, not coincidentally, she is described as "one of that numerous class of females, whose society can raise no other emotion than surprise at their being any men in the world who could like them well enough to marry them." Ouch! When Mrs. Allen interrupts the flirtatious conversation of Catherine and Henry Tilney with her nonsense, Henry cannot resist:

> "My dear Catherine," said she, "do take this pin out of my sleeve; I am afraid it has torn a hole already; I shall be quite sorry if it has, for this is a favourite gown, though it cost but nine shillings a yard."
>
> "That is exactly what I should have guessed it, madam," said Mr. Tilney, looking at the muslin.
>
> "Do you understand muslins, sir?"
>
> "Particularly well; I always buy my own cravats, and am allowed to be an excellent judge. . . ."
>
> "And pray, sir, what do you think of Miss Morland's gown?"
>
> "It is very pretty, madam," said he, gravely examining it; "but I do not think it will wash well; I am afraid it will fray."

And Mrs. Allen has no idea he is not serious! If you have any doubt about the absurdity of extended talk about clothing, just put such chatter into the mouth of a rational person and it will be revealed.

Foolishness is often a companion to fashion-consciousness in Jane Austen's novels: Mrs. Bennet goes on and on about Lydia's wedding clothes without showing as much concern for some assurance that there will in fact be a wedding. Lydia and silly Mrs. Palmer from *Sense and Sensibility* are both described as "wild" to buy new things. Catherine's vain friend Isabella and boastful Mrs. Elton (from *Emma*) also care too much about clothing. While Catherine might lie awake wondering what to wear, she does not *talk* about her wardrobe to others under the ludicrous supposition that the subject will interest them as much. And only the most foolish men in the novels display a concern with such matters—for example, Robert Ferrars, Edward's brother, who rudely keeps Elinor and Marianne waiting to be served in a shop while he chooses, with the greatest of care, a toothpick case.

Perhaps the best example of Austen's attitude towards an excessive concern with clothing appears early in *Pride and Prejudice*. Elizabeth Bennet has walked three miles through the mud to Netherfield to see her sister Jane, who has fallen ill there with a severe cold. Elizabeth—who was warned by her mother that she wouldn't be fit to be seen after such a walk (to which she replied, "I shall be very fit to see Jane—which is all I want")—is abused in her absence by the catty Bingley sisters: "I hope you saw her petticoat, six inches deep in mud, I am absolutely certain; and the gown which had been let down to hide it, not doing its office." But their brother, Mr. Bingley, is having none of it: "I thought Miss Elizabeth Bennet looked remarkably well, when she came into the room this morning. Her dirty petticoat quite escaped my notice." Although the narrator of *Northanger Abbey* knows the statement is one likely to come from a lecturing great-aunt, it nonetheless represents Austen's view: "Excessive solicitude about [dress] often destroys its own aim." And Elizabeth Bennet's lack of self-consciousness about it in this situation is extremely attractive.

83 WHAT DO AUSTEN'S NOVELS SAY ABOUT BEAUTY?

Interestingly, Austen's heroines, with the possible exception of Emma, are not the most beautiful women in her novels. And even Emma, as Mr. Knightley says, is not "personally vain." She has many other flaws, but she wouldn't be very interesting if she spent much time thinking about her beauty. Jane Bennet is more beautiful than her sister Elizabeth, but if she were not also sensible and kind, her looks would soon become less appealing, as we know from examples of other beauties in the novels. Speaking of the Bennets, Mary is "plain," in the euphemism of the day, but her unattractiveness really comes down to her personality—she is pedantic and humorless.

In *Mansfield Park* three beautiful women—Maria and Julia Bertram and Mary Crawford—ultimately fail to win the men they love. As we see so often in Austen's novels, beautiful faces often hide deeply flawed characters. In *Persuasion*, Anne Elliot's sister Elizabeth is so beautiful that even though she has reached the advanced (for the time) age of twenty-nine, their father, a very harsh judge of appearance, still admires her looks. But she is an appallingly vain woman, with "no habits of utility," "no talents or accomplishments'" and no good nature to make the lack of them even tolerable to anyone *but* her father. Catherine Morland's "dear friend" Isabella Thorpe is also beautiful, vain, and a complete phony, winning friends and lovers by superficial means and losing them as her inner ugliness is revealed.

Austen also creates characters who were beautiful young women and by virtue of their beauty won husbands—though the husbands eventually realized that they had been "taken in" by good looks and were now saddled with very foolish lifetime companions. Mrs. Bennet, Mrs. Palmer (from *Sense and Sensibility*), and Lady Bertram fall into this group. And, as we've seen, not only men are taken in by looks—Anne Elliot's mother was infatuated with Sir Walter's good looks, and Wickham's handsome face and smooth manner completely win over Elizabeth Bennet. And if Willoughby, who ensnares—and cruelly dumps—Marianne Dashwood in *Sense and Sensibility* were being described in today's terms, we would say he had "movie-star" good looks.

In her unprecedented (and still unsurpassed) examination of human experience, Austen also shows how a woman's beauty changes according to her mood. Marianne is younger and, at first description, more strikingly beautiful than her sister Elinor, but after Willoughby has disappointed and distressed her and finally broken her heart, her looks deteriorate. Anne Elliot's beauty is also destroyed by heartbreak: She "had been a very pretty girl, but her bloom had vanished early." But when Captain Frederick Wentworth returns, we begin to see Anne's beauty bloom again. Even simple anxiety can destroy beauty: Margaret Watson's features may be good but "the sharp and anxious expression of her face made her beauty in general little felt."

Furthermore, our perception of an individual's beauty changes in any case; that is not fixed in stone either. And as Austen knew so well, perception is at least as powerful as objective reality. In *Mansfield Park*, Mr. Rushworth cannot understand why all the women seem to find Henry Crawford so attractive when he is short and plain to objective eyes. Elinor Dashwood similarly describes how Edward Ferrars's appearance improves "upon acquaintance." At first, "his person can hardly be called handsome" but, she says, "At present, I know him so well, that I think him really handsome; or, at least, almost so."

Even Elizabeth Bennet is only considered "tolerable" by Mr. Darcy and, in the awful words she overhears, "not handsome enough to tempt [*him*]." But she grows on him, and soon he thinks her "one of the handsomest women of [his] acquaintance." And not only pretty girls like Elizabeth become more attractive in the eyes of fastidious men: In *Persuasion*, Mrs. Clay, whose catalogue of unattractive features assures her friend Elizabeth Elliot that the family need not be concerned that their widowed father will consider her for a second wife, strikes the wiser sister Anne as indeed a threat: "There is hardly any personal defect . . . which an agreeable manner might not gradually reconcile one to," she warns. Of course she is correct, even in the case of Sir Walter, who thinks—and speaks—of little besides physical beauty.

Austen shows both that the perception of a woman's beauty is a subjective matter, and that it is greatly influenced by a woman's inner state—which explains why Mr. Bingley never notices Elizabeth Bennet's muddy petticoat when she tramps over to Netherfield, and Mr. Darcy finds that her eyes were "brightened by the exercise." To all this admiration she is admirably indifferent.

PART 6

Untimely Death

84 FOR WHICH NOVEL DO WE HAVE TWO ENDINGS?
Some readers of *Persuasion*, Austen's last completed novel, believe there is still something "incomplete" about it. It is quite a bit shorter than any of the other novels with the exception of the early *Northanger Abbey*, and the William Elliot plot thread has been seen as slightly underdeveloped. Austen started writing *The Elliots*—her working title for *Persuasion*—in 1815, and by the time she completed it, her health had begun to fail. It is possible that she wasn't able to do everything with this novel that she would have liked to do. Still, many people choose *Persuasion* as their favorite Austen novel. While no one could deny that the dazzling *Emma* was more technically brilliant, *Persuasion* is surely the most moving of Austen's novels, and that might explain its special place among them.

Jane Austen finished *Persuasion* on July 18, 1816. Or, rather, she wrote "Finis" at the end of the manuscript but then felt dissatisfied with the ending and rewrote it, discarding one chapter entirely, revising another, and adding new material. Because of this, we have two manuscript chapters—the only original manuscript pages from the finished novels.

The original ending, which is usually appended to modern editions, was first published by Jane's nephew, who included it in the second edition of his *Memoir* in 1871. As he so correctly notes, the manuscript chapters are inferior to the revision but in themselves are quite worthy pieces of writing. In them, Anne Elliot plays a more passive role in letting Captain Wentworth know her feelings for him, which happens when she assures him she is not engaged to William Elliot. Admiral Croft has insisted that Wentworth ask about this because he wants to vacate Kellynch Hall if she and Mr. Elliot have any desire to live there before the Crofts' lease is up. But Anne is the one responsible for the original separation between herself and Wentworth, and she deeply wounded him when she broke off the engagement, so it is fitting that her words should effect their reconciliation in a more active way than this.

The revision contains wonderful new material featuring the Musgroves, and, of course, the breathtaking scene in which Anne and Captain Wentworth communicate their feelings "under cover," as it were. Anne, in a dialogue with Captain Harville, defends the constancy of women in love, declaring that men forget sooner and women love longer even when their love is hopeless. Captain Wentworth hears this and writes a letter to Anne declaring his love while he pretends to be writing to someone else. The suspense is exquisite, and the dialogue perhaps the most gripping in all of Austen's writing. With this new ending, Austen allows quiet Anne Elliot a most eloquent defense of women:

"Men have had every advantage of us in telling their own story. Education has been theirs in so much higher a degree; the pen has been in their hands."

Luckily for us, the pen was now in this woman's hands. Though her health was failing, her creative powers were—miraculously—at their peak when she wrote this scene. As her nephew says of it, "Perhaps it may be thought that she has seldom written anything more brilliant."

85 WHAT DID JANE AUSTEN SAY ABOUT MRS. DARCY?

As we've seen, Jane Austen's characters were largely created in her imagination and not modeled on people the author knew. They became real to Austen, however, just as they've become real to millions of readers. Her nephew tells us that she took a "parental interest" in her characters and that when her nieces and nephews asked, she would tell them what happened to the characters after the novels ended: Miss Steele in *Sense and Sensibility* never caught the doctor; Kitty Bennet married a clergyman near Pemberley, and Mary a clerk in Meryton; Mrs. Norris (in *Mansfield Park*) only gave William Price one pound; and Mr. Woodhouse lived only two years after the marriage of Emma and Mr. Knightley, keeping them at Hartfield—and out of Donwell Abbey—for that long. (So, like Mrs. Churchill, he was sick after all!) Austen revealed the word Frank Churchill placed before Jane Fairfax, which she swept away ("pardon"). It must have been fun to ask Jane Austen such questions!

In 1813, while visiting Henry in London, Jane went with him to several painting exhibitions and wrote the following account to Cassandra, telling her that she had found a portrait of Jane Bennet, now Mrs. Bingley, there:

> *Mrs. Bingley's is exactly herself, size, shaped face, features & sweetness; there never was a greater likeness. She is dressed in a white gown, with green ornaments, which convinces me of what I had always supposed, that green was a favourite colour with her. I dare say Mrs. D. [Darcy] will be in Yellow.*

And then later:

> *I am disappointed, for there was nothing like Mrs. D. at either.—I can only imagine that Mr. D. prizes any Picture of her too much to like it should be exposed to the public eye.—I can imagine he would have that sort of feeling—that mixture of Love, Pride & Delicacy.*

You can hear the affection in her voice. We know what delight she took in Elizabeth Bennet in particular—as who wouldn't? And there is the implication that these characters exist outside of herself, that they might have feelings she doesn't know about.

It is wonderful to have these remarks about her characters from the creator of them herself, but stories about what happened to them beyond the final chapters of the novels by no means ended with her. Since Jane

Austen's death, and particularly in recent years, many readers have imagined continued lives for Mr. and Mrs. Darcy and many of Austen's other characters. Of course, it is most gratifying and amusing to have the author's own authoritative descriptions of the continued lives of her "children," even if they are only brief offhand remarks meant, as so much of her talk was, purely for the amusement of her family.

86 ANNA AUSTEN

"Now that you are become an Aunt, you are a person of some consequence & must excite great Interest whatever You do. I have always maintained the importance of Aunts as much as possible," wrote Jane Austen to her little niece Caroline upon the birth of Anna-Jemima, the first child of Caroline's half-sister Anna. And, indeed, the role of aunt was a very important one to Austen. Her nieces Anna and Fanny were the two of her brothers' children closest to her, and they present an interesting study in contrasting personalities.

Anna, the daughter of James Austen, was the second grandchild and Mrs. Austen's favorite. Because her mother died when Anna was just two, the little girl went to live at Steventon with her grandmother and her aunts Cassandra and Jane, and this naturally created a special intimacy. Moreover, Anna was a pretty, passionate, very intelligent girl, but her unpredictability kept her family a little nervous about what she might do next. Jane, who loved her dearly, nonetheless spoke of "much unsteadiness" in her character. Once James remarried, Anna had problems getting along with her stepmother. She impetuously became engaged at the age of sixteen and then broke off the engagement after securing her family's reluctant acceptance of it. She eventually married Ben Lefroy, the son of Jane's old friend Mrs. Lefroy and cousin of her old flame Tom. With the same families turning up again and again, we see how limited the circle of acquaintance was in the country.

Jane had seen more than enough of women being dragged down physically and actually killed by childbearing, so once Anna started having babies, Jane began to worry about her. When Anna was pregnant with her third child, and not feeling up to a walk, Jane wrote to Fanny, "Anna has not a chance of escape. . . . Poor animal, she will be worn out before she is thirty.—I am very sorry for her." (Anna apparently suffered a miscarriage.)

Anna liked to write stories too (not surprising in a bright child who listened to *Pride and Prejudice* being read aloud in the Steventon rectory when it was still in its early form) and Jane encouraged her and advised her, reading her work and urging her not to use phrases such as "vortex of Dissipation," which she condemned as "thorough novel slang." Imagine having Jane Austen as your creative writing teacher! Anna's daughter Fanny tells a touching story that shows how much Anna loved her. Once Aunt Jane had died, Anna lost interest in the novel she had been writing, titled *Which is the Heroine?* Aunt Jane's sympathy, Fanny writes, "which had made the great charm of the occupation was gone and the sense of the loss made it painful to write." Not only did Anna abandon the manuscript, but "in a fit of despondency" she burnt it. Even in later years you can see Anna's sensitive, passionate, impulsive nature in this act.

As Mr. Knightley said of Emma, "There is an anxiety, a curiosity in what one feels for Emma," and the young Anna Austen seems to have excited the same feelings in her family. Indeed, it has been said that within the family, Anna was thought to have been the model for Emma. But Emma Woodhouse is much cooler than Anna ever appears to have been, and we might also detect some of Anna in the very different Marianne Dashwood's deep feeling and volatility—although Anna is too young to have influenced *Elinor and Marianne*, which, as mentioned earlier, was the original version of *Sense and Sensibility*. In any case, as we've noted, although certain traits might have been suggested by Anna, Jane Austen's characters were creations, not imitations.

Anna Lefroy, née Austen, was never dull—and there is the additional interesting fact that she married a man with the same last name as her Aunt Jane's own lost love.

87 FANNY KNIGHT

Fanny, the first Austen grandchild, the daughter of Jane's brother Edward, was born, like Anna, when Jane was seventeen. Since Edward had been adopted by the wealthy Knights, Fanny grew up in luxury, with loving parents and many brothers and sisters. (When Mrs. Knight died in 1812, Edward's family took the name. "How I hate it!!!!" Fanny wrote.)

When Fanny was fifteen, her mother, Elizabeth, died shortly after giving birth to her eleventh child. As the eldest, Fanny essentially took over her mother's role as mistress of Godmersham. Fanny was a great diarist, so we have many detailed accounts of the time she spent with her aunt, both there and at Chawton.

After settling his mother and sisters in his property in Hampshire, Edward enjoyed his visits there so much that he decided to use Chawton House himself instead of renting it out. This meant Fanny could spend even more time with Aunt Jane, both at the Cottage and at the impressive Great House, and the two became even closer. In a letter to Cassandra in 1808, Jane wrote, "I found [Fanny] in the summer just what you describe, almost another Sister, & could not have supposed that a neice would ever have been so much to me. She is quite after one's own heart."

Just as Jane wrote to Anna giving advice about writing, she wrote to Fanny advising her on how to proceed with various suitors at different times. Fanny has expressed a change of heart about one of these, and in a letter Jane goes over all of the many things in the gentleman's favor—"advantages which do not often meet in one person." She then turns around and advises her niece "not to think of accepting him unless you really do like him. Anything is to be preferred or endured rather than marrying without Affection." In this advice we see the attitude Austen would give to her heroines, and act upon in her own life.

A few years later Fanny still has not married and again seeks Aunt Jane's advice, this time about another man. "Do not be in a hurry," Aunt Jane tells her. "[D]epend upon it, the right Man will come at last; you

101 Things You Didn't Know about Jane Austen

will in the course of the next two or three years, meet with somebody more generally unexceptionable than anyone you have yet known, who will love you as warmly as ever *He* did, & who will so completely attach you, that you will feel you never really loved before." This seems to be an extremely romantic point of view! But, to balance it out, Austen adds some shrewd practical advice that you might not expect: She advises Fanny not to begin having children too early in life. If she puts off "Mothering" for a while she will be "young in Constitution, spirits, figure & countenance," because labor and nursing are aging. Jane Austen had seen too closely the downside of all those children in the Austen family.

When Fanny was an old woman, this "favorite niece" made some remarks about her aunt in a letter to her sister Marianne that many of Austen's fans see as a betrayal. She said the Hampshire Austens "were not rich and the people around with whom they chiefly mixed, were not at all high bred . . . and *they* of course tho' superior in *mental powers & cultivation* were on the same level as far as *refinement* goes." Fanny goes on to say that her aunts' visits to Godmersham introduced them to the customs of good society. Of course, this was said in a private letter to her sister at a time of life when her mind was said to be confused, and while it does not evince a *blind* devotion to her aunt, it doesn't prove Fanny didn't love her. In fact, from all the evidence, Jane and Fanny had a very strong bond.

88 JANE AUSTEN'S RELIGION

Henry Austen wrote of his sister that "her opinions accorded strictly with those of our Established Church," and that seems to be true. With the exception of *Mansfield Park*, Jane Austen's novels contain little direct discussion of religion. As befits the daughter, granddaughter, and sister of clergymen in the Church of England, she took religion seriously in her life without, however, often bringing it into her art. There, as Richard Whately, later Archbishop of Dublin, wrote, it is "not at all obtrusive."

Austen read sermons with interest and she composed devout, if conventional, prayers. She kept her religion for the most part quietly and privately. "I do not like the Evangelicals," she says flatly in a letter to Cassandra, no doubt objecting to their *very* obtrusive style of Christianity. Yet, a few years later, in one of the letters of advice to Fanny in which she weighs the pros and cons of her niece's suitor, she says she does not object to the possibility of the young man's becoming an Evangelical: "I am by no means convinced that we ought not all to be Evangelicals, & am at least persuaded that they who are so from Reason & Feeling, must be happiest & safest." With irony, she adds, "don't be frightened by the idea of his acting more strictly up to the precepts of the New Testament than others." Austen was very far from objecting to the *piety* of Evangelicals—she was herself devout, but quietly so.

An interesting reference to religion appears also in a letter to Martha Lloyd pertaining to war with America. Henry has told Jane such a war could not be won and she writes, "I place my hope of better things on a claim to the protection of Heaven, as a Religious Nation, a Nation inspite of much Evil improving in Religion, which I cannot beleive the Americans to possess." It is not the kind of statement, mixing politics and religion, you would expect to hear from any of Austen's heroines, with the possible exception of Fanny Price.

89 *SANDITON*: A GLIMPSE OF UNCHARTED LAND

Although *Persuasion* was Jane Austen's last completed novel, she did leave a fragment of another one. In January 1817 she began working on a new book, and the last date on the manuscript is March 18, 1817. She died exactly four months later. While *Persuasion* is romantic and contains a good deal of melancholy, *Sanditon* is briskly comic. It is hard to believe it was written while the author's health must have been declining rapidly. Neither the style nor the subject matter betray that fact.

One of the things Austen appears to be satirizing in *Sanditon* is, in sweeping terms, the spirit of change. Innovation and commercialization, the story *seems* to say, are ridiculous and wrong and bad for the country. Yet, although the satire frequently aims at those targets, Austen actually draws a picture in which they appear in a positive light at least as often, and it is not at all clear that she didn't enjoy and welcome such change as much as she mistrusted it.

The story begins when Mr. and Mrs. Parker's carriage overturns after they are "induced by business" to leave the high road and take a "very rough lane." Mr. Parker is not at all prudent, but if Jane Austen disapproves of his eagerness and optimism it is a purely theoretical disapproval, for she has made him an entirely likeable character. He is a "complete enthusiast" on the subject of Sanditon: "The success of Sanditon as a small, fashionable bathing place was the object, for which he seemed to live." He and the other principal landowner in this seaside village considered it "a profitable speculation" and have been building it up and pushing it as the hot new resort. Sanditon is "his mine, his lottery, his speculation and his hobby horse; his occupation his hope and his futurity." When the carriage carries the Parkers back to Sanditon, they pass their old house—the house of his forefathers—a mile and three-quarters inland and Mr. Parker notes how "Our ancestors . . . always built in a hole." His wife looks back regretfully at the pleasant, shady garden and thinks how the neighbors didn't even feel a recent storm whereas they, in their new house with an ocean view, were rocked in their beds. Mr. Parker, whose spirits are irrepressible, responds that they have "all the grandeur of the storm, with less real danger." Although this is a new vogue, this building on the ocean instead of more securely inland, and Mr. Parker is quick to leave the ancestral home—and all its history and tradition—without a backward glance, can any reader fault him for it? We've seen how much Jane Austen herself loved the sea. Although some good old things will be lost with innovation, some change is actually progress.

Mr. Parker is so much a man of the moment that he rather regrets having named his new home Trafalgar House because "Waterloo is more the thing now." When he looks in the window of a shoemaker's shop and sees

"Blue shoes, and nankin boots!" and cries "This is new within the month. . . . Glorious indeed!—Well, I think I *have* done something in my day," he might be ridiculous, but there are so many contrasting examples of inertia and extreme prudence in *Sanditon* that, coming from kindly, cheerful Mr. Parker, all these outbursts are quite forgivable.

Another subject the story addresses is hypochondria, and here there is no conflict in the author's satire. It is a surprising subject for a dying woman to choose, and one wonders where Austen would have gone with it. So much in *Sanditon* is entirely new in Austen's writing that it is impossible to know how the story would have unfolded. Alas, the author became too ill to continue writing, so we will never know.

90 WHAT KILLED JANE AUSTEN?

On March 23, 1817, five days after laying aside the manuscript of *Sanditon* for good, Jane Austen wrote to her niece Fanny: "I certainly have not been well for many weeks, & about a week ago I was very poorly, I have had a good deal of fever at times & indifferent nights, but am considerably better now, & recovering my Looks a little, which have been bad enough, black & white & every wrong colour." In addition to fevers and facial discoloration, Austen also suffered from gastrointestinal distress. She often felt weak—sometimes very weak—and one of her early complaints was of back pain. These symptoms grew more and more severe over the next few months, although there were periods in which she rallied. Her niece Caroline tells of how her aunt would arrange three chairs for herself to lie on, calling them "*her* sofa," and leave the one sofa in the room vacant because Mrs. Austen liked to lie on it after she had been working in the garden. Caroline pestered her aunt until she revealed why she wouldn't use the real sofa even when it was empty, as it often was, and Jane's reply was, "If *she* ever used the sofa, Grandmama would be leaving it for *her*, and would not lie down, as she did now, whenever she felt inclined."

Mrs. Austen's brother, James Leigh-Perrot, died on March 28. The Austens had high hopes for this rich, childless uncle's will, but he left his entire estate to his widow, with £1,000 to be paid to each of the Austen children after *her* death. Jane wrote to her brother Charles that "the shock of my Uncle's Will brought on a relapse." In May, Jane was taken to Winchester to be treated by doctors there. Although she had good days, her doctor, Mr. Lyford, held out no hope.

On July 17 Cassandra and Mary Austen, James's wife, saw Jane's condition change. Mr. Lyford pronounced her close to death, saying a large blood vessel had burst, and gave her laudanum to ease her suffering. Cassandra asked her if she wanted anything and she replied, "Nothing but death." She lost consciousness and at half past four in the morning, with her head on a pillow in Cassandra's lap, she died. Jane Austen was forty-one years old.

In a 1964 article in the *British Medical Journal*, Sir Zachary Cope diagnosed Austen's fatal illness, based on the record of her symptoms, as Addison's disease, a tuberculosis of the adrenal glands. A letter in response to this by F. mA. Bevan suggests that a lymphoma such as Hodgkin's disease

was the likelier cause of her death. There is continued debate and speculation about what Jane Austen's fatal illness really was, and no doubt there
always will be.

91 JANE AUSTEN'S WILL

On April 27, 1817, Jane Austen, almost always practical, saw what
might be coming and made out her will. It was short and simple. She left
£50 to Henry, who was not only her favorite brother but now really needed
the money after his bankruptcy. Surprisingly, she also left £50 to Madame
Bigeon. Everything else went to Cassandra, who was the executrix.

As a woman Cassandra could not attend Jane's funeral, and she watched
as the procession disappeared from view around the corner. She saw that
mementoes—locks of hair and modest items that had belonged to Jane—
were sent to Fanny and a few others. She also assured Fanny that Jane had
been "better known to you than to any human being besides myself,"
maintaining the family view of that special relationship. (However, Anna's
daughter seems justified in claiming that none of the nieces mourned
Aunt Jane as deeply as did her mother.) As for Cassandra herself, she had
behaved stoically all those years earlier when her fiancé died, but surely
this bereavement was even worse. She and Jane had been extraordinarily
close their whole lives. She once again kept her composure but expressed
the depth of her grief in these words to Fanny: "I *have* lost a treasure, such
a Sister, such a friend as never can have been surpassed, —She was the sun

of my life, the gilder of every pleasure, the soother of every sorrow, I had not a thought concealed from her, & it is as if I had lost a part of myself." It is hard to imagine a more beautiful tribute coming even from the pen of Jane Austen.

92 WHAT SECRETS DO JANE AUSTEN'S LETTERS REVEAL?

When we think of the number of ways available to us today by which we can communicate over distance with family, friends, lovers, and those with whom we have business to conduct, and then consider that Jane Austen had just one way, the handwritten letter, we realize that she must have written and received a tremendous number of letters in her lifetime. Where are those letters now?

Although Jane and her sister Cassandra were together most of the time, they were frequently separated, most often when one or the other was staying at the home of a brother. The bulk of the letters of Jane's that we have are those written to Cassandra. Their niece Caroline writes, "My Aunt looked them over and burnt the greater part, (as she told me), 2 or 3 years before her own death—She left, or *gave* some as legacies to the Nieces—but of those that *I* have seen, several had portions cut out." Although we cringe to read this, the Austens valued discretion and honored privacy. No doubt some things in the letters were just too personal for public display. Moreover, Cassandra was exhibiting a delicate regard for the feelings of others in removing, one way or the other, negative remarks about family members that might have been hurtful—although a few of these slipped by for us to read today. Deirdre Le Faye, the editor of the most recent edition of the letters, explains that Cassandra's censorship involved primarily the destruction of whole letters, and that in the surviving letters the excision of words is minor and seems to have occurred when Austen spoke too openly about physical ailments or symptoms.

After the death of Frank Austen, his daughter Fanny destroyed Jane's letters to him, which he had carefully kept for so long. (He had outlived his sister by almost fifty years.) In 1884, Fanny Knight's son Lord Brabourne (Fanny had married a rich baronet, Sir Edward Knatchbull, three years after her aunt's death) published the letters that had been in his mother's possession. In their editing we see a Victorian concern with gentility. For example, the line, "I have a very good eye at an Adultress"—among others—is suppressed.

So what do we have, then? There are around 160 letters extant, and most contain everyday family news, much of it about small domestic matters—new furniture, dress material, plants in the garden, weather. The health and welfare of various family members is related and discussed, seriously or comically as the situation dictates. This being Jane Austen, the playful remarks are imaginative and witty. There is gossip about neighbors, some of it quite sharp. Some rude, even vulgar jokes have survived. Austen sometimes reveals exasperation and depression, sometimes optimism and joy. The letters contain frequent expressions of deep affection for family and friends that are eloquent and moving.

As R. W. Chapman, the great editor of Jane Austen's writings, points out, Jane's letters to Cassandra are more focused on the "business of news," whereas other correspondents more fully inspire the "flow of fancy." Indeed, the letters to her nieces and her nephew James-Edward are delightfully imaginative and amusing. Even the trivial everyday matters found in the letters are fascinating reading for anyone with an interest in Jane Austen.

93 POSTHUMOUS PUBLICATION: *NORTHANGER ABBEY* AND *PERSUASION*

Despite repeated efforts, Jane Austen did not see *Northanger Abbey*—originally called *Susan*—published in her lifetime. Henry had negotiated with the publisher Crosby for the manuscript's return in 1816—thirteen years after it had been purchased and then not published. (Only after he had possession of the manuscript, repurchased for the original selling price of £10, did Henry reveal that the author was the same as she who had written *Pride and Prejudice*. Ha!) Once the manuscript of *Susan* was back in her hands, Austen went through it, changing the heroine's name to Catherine. In 1816 she wrote the "Advertisement by the Authoress" in which she says the book was finished in 1803 and that, since then, "places, manners, books, and opinions have undergone considerable changes." She takes three sentences (out of five) to criticize Crosby—though not by name—for his nonaction: "That any bookseller should think it worth while to purchase what he did not think it worth while to publish seems extraordinary." Obviously, the business still irritated her.

In March of 1817 she wrote to her niece Fanny: "Miss Catherine is put upon the Shelve for the present, and I do not know that she will ever come out;—but I have a something ready for Publication, which may perhaps appear about a twelvemonth hence." That something was *The Elliots*; that is, *Persuasion*. But four months after writing this letter Jane Austen was dead, and it was up to others to see that these two novels got published. As her nephew writes, speaking of the continued lives of his aunt's characters as she used to playfully reveal them, "Of the good people in 'Northanger Abbey' and 'Persuasion' we know nothing more than what is written: for before those works were published their author had been taken away from us, and all such amusing communications had ceased forever."

Henry and Cassandra decided on the titles *Northanger Abbey* and *Persuasion* for the two novels, and Henry negotiated a deal with Jane's previous publisher, John Murray. *Northanger Abbey* and *Persuasion* were published together in December 1817, although the title page says 1818. 1,750 copies were printed. Included with the novels were the "Advertisement" and a "Biographical Notice of the Author" written by Henry, which was the first effort to make public the details of Jane Austen's life. It is a somewhat idealized portrait, emphasizing Jane's sweetness of temper, Christian faith and virtue, and her genius. Henry describes his sister's appearance, accomplishments, wit, and literary taste. According to Henry, "so much did she shrink from notoriety, that no accumulation of fame would have induced her, had she lived, to affix her name to any productions of her pen." What on earth would Jane Austen think of the fame her name has accumulated in the almost two centuries that have passed since her beloved brother wrote that sentence?

94 JANE AUSTEN REMEMBERED

When we read the memoirs of Jane Austen written by family members, certain aspects of her personality stand out. One of these is her extraordinarily wonderful way with children. She was evidently very skillful in games that required manual dexterity, but the talent that shines most brightly in accounts of her interactions with children is, not surprisingly, her skill at spinning stories for and with them.

Anna, James's daughter, writes, "Aunt Jane was the general favorite with children; her ways with them being so playful, & her long circumstantial stories so delightful! These were continued from time to time, & begged for of course at all possible or impossible occasions; woven, as she proceeded out of nothing, but her own happy talent for invention." Anna tells how during the period when she lived close to Chawton she would spend a good bit of time visiting her aunts and having playful conversations with Jane, "one piece of absurdity leading to another, till Aunt Cassandra fatigued with her own share of laughter would exclaim 'How *can* you both be so foolish?' & beg us to leave off." This little story also nicely illustrates the difference in personality between the sisters, although Anna adds interestingly that Aunt Jane, when grave, "was *very* grave" and that

Cassandra's disposition might in fact have been "the most equally cheerful of the two."

Anna's half-sister Caroline, in words that their brother James-Edward borrows for his longer *Memoir*, describes how Aunt Jane would gossip most entertainingly about the neighbors, but "it was her own nonsense that gave zest to the gossip. . . . The laugh she occasionally raised was by imagining for her neighbors impossible contingencies—by relating in prose or verse some trifling incident coloured to her own fancy, or in writing a history of what they had said or done, that *could* deceive nobody." This incisive description could serve equally well for Jane's comic technique—if we can call it that—in her letters. There too the gossip itself is trifling but given zest and interest by the writer's imagination.

Caroline tells how she and other cousins would listen to Aunt Jane as she told "the most delightful stories chiefly of Fairyland, and her Fairies had all characters of their own—The tale was invented, I am sure, at the moment, and was sometimes continued for 2 or 3 days, if occasion served." Aunt Jane was also the one the children went to when they needed any props or costumes for their games of "make-believe." And, as she had encouraged Anna with her writing, so she did the same with James-Edward (called Edward in the family) and little Caroline when they in turn began writing novels.

It is no wonder that Jane Austen's nieces and nephews felt so deeply the loss of their aunt, who entered into their feelings and thoughts as few other adults did. Caroline says, "*Not* to have found Aunt Jane at Chawton, *would* have been a blank indeed!" She recounts that one of her cousins would visit Aunt Cassandra at the cottage after Jane's death and be sadly disappointed because he always went there expecting to be very happy, but "all its peculiar pleasures were gone." Anna also tells how she would save things up to tell her aunt—things that no one else would understand and enjoy in the same way.

To echo a sentiment expressed by Anna, if only one of Jane Austen's stories of Fairyland could be recovered!

Part 7

Austen and Popular Culture: From the Eighteenth Century to the Twenty-First

95 WHO WERE JANE AUSTEN'S FAVORITE NOVELISTS?
Mr. Austen's library at Steventon was extensive, containing five hundred books, and we know that the rectory was a congenial place for those with literary inclinations. Henry Austen recalls of Jane: "It is difficult to say at what age she was not intimately acquainted with the merits and defects of the best essays and novels in the English language." None of the novelists Austen read and admired are today considered as great as she is (though some critics still hold out for the sublime Henry Fielding), and certainly none are as popular. As for Austen's favorite novel—it is probably not much read outside of graduate programs in English literature, if there. James-Edward, echoing Henry, writes, "Her knowledge of Richardson's

works was such as no one is likely again to acquire. . . . Every circumstance narrated in Sir Charles Grandison . . . was familiar to her." Samuel Richardson's *Sir Charles Grandison* was the favorite, and Austen makes an amusing reference to it in *Northanger Abbey*. Isabella Thorpe is surprised to learn that Mrs. Morland reads that novel, and—repeating the opinion of Miss Andrews—Isabella calls it "amazing horrid," adding "I thought it had not been readable." Catherine, however, finds it "very entertaining." As we know, Catherine has a lot to learn, but she has natural good taste, which is here contrasted with Isabella's—or Miss Andrews's—lack of literary sensibility.

Austen said of her family that they were "great Novel-readers & not ashamed of being so" at a time when novels weren't considered serious literature. Although she is making fun of certain novelistic conventions in *Northanger Abbey*, it is in that book that she also defends novels such as *Cecilia*, *Camilla*, and *Belinda*—the first two by Fanny Burney and the last by Maria Edgeworth, two of Jane's other favorite novelists—as examples of works in which "the greatest powers of the mind are displayed, in which the most thorough knowledge of human nature, the happiest delineation of its varieties, the liveliest effusions of wit and humour are conveyed to the world in the best chosen language." The bad taste of the Thorpe family is shown again when Isabella's brother John calls *Camilla* "stupid," "unnatural," and "the horridest nonsense." To understand the contemporary stature of these two novelists, consider this (almost incredible) opinion expressed by James-Edward, again following Henry: If anyone "had known that we, in our secret thoughts, classed her with Madame D'Arblay [Burney] or Miss

Edgeworth, or even with some other novel writers of the day whose names are now [in 1870] scarcely remembered, they would have considered it an amusing instance of family conceit."

Austen also read Fielding (his novels and plays); Laurence Sterne; Shakespeare, of course; and other women writers such as Charlotte Lennox, Charlotte Smith, and Hannah Cowley. Obviously, she read the Gothic novels she mocks in *Northanger Abbey*. Some playwrights were made familiar to her through the Steventon theatricals if not through her father's library. Samuel Johnson was her favorite prose writer, and we can hear the influence of his style in many of her sentences—elegant and rational, but with her own witty, even nonsensical twist. Henry tells us that she admired William Gilpin's writing on the picturesque. Whatever Jane Austen enjoyed and admired in these writers and others—those who are still widely read and those whose names are almost completely unknown today—she did not copy their works but began to develop and display her own unique style at a prodigiously early age.

96 WHICH POETS DID SHE LIKE?

William Cowper, George Crabbe, and Sir Walter Scott were some of Jane Austen's favorite poets. It's interesting to see what the taste in poetry of some of Jane Austen's heroines says about them.

Marianne, in *Sense and Sensibility*, complains about the way Edward Ferrars reads Cowper aloud: "To hear those beautiful lines which have frequently almost driven me wild, pronounced with such impenetrable calmness, such dreadful indifference! . . . [I]f he is not to be animated by Cowper!" Cowper's meditative poetry celebrated the beauty of nature. He is often considered an early Romantic poet, and as such would particularly appeal to Marianne. Later Elinor will tease her about Willoughby: "You know what he thinks of Cowper and Scott; you are certain of his estimating their beauties as he ought, and you have received every assurance of his admiring Pope no more than is proper." Scott's poetry was also romantic, whereas the great eighteenth-century poet Alexander Pope wrote verse in an entirely different style—one that would be considered too cool and rational by a girl with Marianne's sensibility. She could never be driven wild by Pope! No matter how much Jane Austen criticizes Marianne, we should note that she gives this heroine her own taste in poetry.

Austen's romantic heroines—Marianne, Fanny, and Anne—are the ones who are most passionate about poetry. Elizabeth Bennet prefers to joke about it: "I wonder who first discovered the efficacy of poetry in driving away love! . . . [I]f it be only a slight, thin sort of inclination, I am convinced that one good sonnet will starve it entirely away." Fanny Price, on the other hand, recalls lines of poetry to express her thoughts and feelings. When she learns that Mr. Rushworth is eager to have the avenue of trees on his estate cut down, she says to Edmund, "Cut down an avenue! What a pity! Does not it make you think of Cowper? 'Ye fallen avenues, once more I mourn your fate unmerited.'" And when Fanny finds the chapel at Sotherton to be far less grand and evocative than she had imagined, she quotes from Sir Walter Scott's "The Lay of the Last Minstrel" to express how far the chapel falls short of her ideal. (Fanny also reads Crabbe and Samuel Johnson.) But Fanny's expectations are, like Marianne's, too heavily influenced by her reading, for Scott's poems, with their extravagantly romantic medieval subjects, are very far from reality indeed.

In *Persuasion*, Anne Elliot is happy to discuss the poetry of Scott and Byron with Captain Benwick, who is mourning the death of his fiancée, Fanny Harville. Captain Benwick:

> *shewed himself so intimately acquainted with all the tenderest songs of the one poet, and all the impassioned descriptions of hopeless agony of the other; he repeated, with such tremulous feeling, the various lines which imaged a broken heart, or a mind destroyed by wretchedness, and looked so entirely as if he meant to be understood, that she ventured to hope he did not always read only poetry; and to say, that she thought it was the misfortune of poetry, to be seldom safely enjoyed by those who enjoyed it completely; and that the strong feelings which alone could estimate it truly, were the very feelings which ought to taste it but sparingly.*

Anne recommends to Captain Benwick that he read a little more prose.

Anne is as romantic as Marianne and just as susceptible to the sweet, melancholy autumn scene before her, and all the poetry it brings to mind, but when she hears Captain Wentworth's voice, she "could not immediately fall into a quotation again."

97 DID JANE AUSTEN AND SIR WALTER SCOTT EVER MEET? Jane Austen admired Sir Walter Scott's writing and he hers, but they never met. Austen did not hobnob with the literary crowd. As Henry Austen tells us, she would have been pained by publicly playing the role of "authoress" and she avoided any trace of literary lionization.

Scott's reputation at the time was much higher than Austen's. Even her nephew refers to Scott as a "greater genius than my aunt." John Murray, Austen's publisher, asked Scott if he would like to review *Emma* for the influential *Quarterly Review*, adding "It wants incident and romance, does it not?" Scott gave it a good, if not tremendous review, praising it for "copying from nature as she really exists in the common walks of life." He is reminded, he says, of the "merits of the Flemish school of painting."

Austen's response to Murray after reading the review was, "The Authoress of *Emma* has no reason I think to complain of her treatment . . . except in the total omission of *Mansfield Park*.—I cannot but be sorry that so clever a Man as the Reveiwer of *Emma*, should consider it as unworthy of being noticed." Scott's review was anonymous and we don't know if Austen knew he was the reviewer. When his novel *Waverly* was published anonymously she did—somehow—know right away that he was the author.

James-Edward Austen-Leigh, in comparing Scott's review, written in 1815, with a glowing review of Austen's novels by Richard Whately, written in 1821, shrewdly concludes that in the intervening years "these works had been read and reread by many leaders in the literary world. The public taste was forming itself all this time, and 'grew by what it fed on.'"

In other words, by reading Austen's novels, readers were becoming better able to appreciate Austen's novels, which came on the literary scene with no precedents. So, he continues, "each Reviewer represented fairly enough the prevailing opinions of readers in the year when each wrote." This idea that reading Austen created in readers the ability to appreciate her extraordinary and totally new novels can be considered with regard to just one reviewer, Walter Scott.

Austen-Leigh notes that his aunt's novels "gain rather than lose by frequent perusals." When we turn to Scott's journal entry from March 14, 1816, written ten years after his review of *Emma*, we find this:

> *Also read again, and for the third time at least, Miss Austen's very finely written novel of "Pride and Prejudice." That young lady has a talent for describing the involvements and feelings and characters of ordinary life, which is to me the most wonderful I have ever met with. The Big Bow-Wow strain I can do myself like any now going; but the exquisite touch which renders ordinary common-place things and characters interesting from the truth of the description and the sentiment is denied to me.*

How much more effusive in his praise is Sir Walter now than when he wrote for John Murray!

When James-Edward visited the place where Scott had lived and took the author's personal "well-worn" copies of Jane Austen's novels into his hands, at a time when both writers were dead, he wished "that she had lived to know what such men thought of her powers, and how gladly they would have cultivated a personal acquaintance with her."

And what conversations those two would have had! With a nod to his aunt's distaste for public attention, he adds, "I do not think that it would at all have impaired the modest simplicity of her character; or that we should have lost our own dear 'Aunt Jane' in the blaze of literary fame."

98 VICTORIANS AND OTHERS

Jane Austen's reputation did not take off immediately. Her works were out of print in England during the 1820s. She was not as popular as Scott, Thackeray, or Dickens early in the Victorian period. Scott's warm praise of Austen in his journal appeared in J. G. Lockhart's *The Life of Scott*, published in 1837–38, so the many who admired him learned his high opinion of her. Critical acclaim also came from other important writers. In 1843 Thomas Macaulay said Austen came close to Shakespeare. George Henry Lewes, who would later live as a husband with George Eliot, praised Austen, calling her "the most *real* . . . the most truthful, charming, humourous, pureminded, quick-witted, and unexaggerated of writers." He names her and Fielding as "the greatest novelists in our language." Lewes urges Charlotte Brontë to learn from Austen, and in January 1848 she writes back expressing her puzzlement: "Why do you like Miss Austen so very much?" she asks him. Here is Brontë's famous, dismissive assessment of *Pride and Prejudice*:

> *An accurate daguerreotyped portrait of a commonplace face; a carefully fenced, highly cultivated garden, with neat borders and delicate flowers; but no glance of a bright vivid physiognomy, no open country, no fresh air, no blue hill, no bonny beck [stream]. I should hardly like to live with her ladies and gentlemen, in their elegant but confined houses.*

Brontë flatly rejects the idea that Jane Austen is "great." Ralph Waldo Emerson also cannot understand "why people hold Miss Austen's novels at so high a rate," finding them "without genius, wit, or knowledge of the world." George Eliot, however, did learn from Austen, as did Anthony Trollope, Henry James, and countless others.

Once James-Edward Austen-Leigh's *Memoir* was published in 1870, Austen's popularity grew. When Alfred, Lord Tennyson, the great poet laureate, was visiting Lyme, and friends wanted to show him where the Duke of Monmouth had landed in 1685 (an important historical event), he reportedly cried out: "Don't talk to me of the Duke of Monmouth. Show me the exact spot where Louisa Musgrove fell," referring to a major dramatic scene in *Persuasion*.

In the twentieth century, E. M. Forster wrote of his devotion to Austen, and Virginia Woolf praised her, noting that "of all great writers she is the most difficult to catch in the act of greatness." Rudyard Kipling wrote "The Janeites," a story published in 1924 about British soldiers in World War I who share a love of Jane Austen. C. S. Lewis was also a fan.

Today, countless writers of all kinds name Jane Austen as their favorite novelist. J. K. Rowling and P. D. James are just two well-known examples.

In both popular and critical acclaim she has far surpassed all who have ever debated her merits.

99 Just how many film, television, and stage adaptations of Austen novels have there been?

Too many to count! Furthermore, any number printed here would quickly become outdated because there are numerous new productions in the works at this moment. Obviously, Austen's novels are endlessly appealing, and interest in them appears to grow ever stronger. While some fans were convinced that the 1995 BBC production of *Pride and Prejudice* was definitive, and that no one could surpass Colin Firth in portraying Mr. Darcy, 2005 saw the release of a new version, with a very different sensibility and a very different Mr. Darcy. The superb film adaptation of *Persuasion* that appeared in 1995 was considered the best film of the year by at least one major critic—Michael Medved—and yet 2007 will see a new Anne Elliot and a new Captain Wentworth finding their way back to each other on the windswept Cobb at Lyme Regis and in the elegant drawing rooms of Bath. There are new stage productions and musicals every year. Many Austen fans find some adaptations overly romanticized, sweetened, simplified, and/or vulgarized, but others become as passionate about them as about the original works (sometimes even more so).

And that is only the direct adaptations of Austen's novels. Many other books and movies are inspired by Austen's works, from *Emma*-derived

Clueless to *Bridget Jones's Diary*—with its own Mr. Darcy (Colin Firth again) and a Wickham stand-in played against type by Hugh Grant—to Bollywood's *Bride and Prejudice*. Then there are books, such as the hit novel *The Jane Austen Book Club* and the Jane Austen Mystery series. There are self-help books based on Austen's writings, such as *Dear Jane Austen: A Heroine's Guide to Life and Love* (written by this author). There are thousands of works of "fan fiction," stories of varying length and quality based on Austen's novels and featuring her characters. There are also thousands of books, articles, and conference papers containing critical analysis of Austen.

Many fans of Jane Austen band together to pledge their allegiance to their favorite author and meet to celebrate and discuss her. The largest and most important of these are the Jane Austen Societies. The Jane Austen Society of North America has three thousand members, and there are Jane Austen Societies in the United Kingdom, Australia, and South America. Jane Austen's House, Chawton Cottage, is now a museum where visitors can see the room Jane shared with Cassandra, and the table where she wrote and revised her novels. The Jane Austen Centre in Bath holds a Jane Austen Festival attended by large numbers of fans every year, and thousands more Janeites are pursuing their interest in Austen on Web sites such as "Austenblog."

One thing is clear: what Shakespeare—the only writer who can justly be compared to Austen—wrote of Cleopatra holds for Jane, too: "Age cannot wither her, nor custom stale / Her infinite variety. "

100 "The little bit (two Inches wide) of Ivory"

When Jane Austen heard that several chapters of the novel her nephew James-Edward was working on were missing, she wrote to him playfully: "I do not think however that any theft of that sort would be really very useful to me. What should I do with your strong, manly, spirited Sketches, full of Variety & Glow?—How could I possibly join them on to the little bit (two Inches wide) of Ivory on which I work with so fine a Brush, as produces little effect after much labour?" She did not write in what Scott called "the Big Bow-Wow strain"—strong, manly, and entertaining, yet in its way as far removed from common life as the Gothic novels of Austen's youth, which, as Catherine Morland discovered, were "charming" yet "it was not in them perhaps that human nature . . . was to be looked for." In her youth, as we've seen, Austen mocked the absurd characters and events she found in novels, amusing herself and her family by exaggerating even further the lack of probability in those aspects of her own stories. In 1813 she dismissed a new novel called *Self-Control*, by Mary Brunton—in which the heroine escapes the villain by floating down the river in a canoe—calling it "an excellently-meant, elegantly-written Work, without anything of Nature or Probability in it. I declare I do not know whether Laura's passage down the American river, is not the most natural, possible, every-day thing she ever does." In another letter she jokes that she will write an imitation of that novel, but "my Heroine shall not merely be wafted down an American river in a boat by herself, she shall cross the Atlantic in the same way, & never stop till she reaches Gravesend." Jane Austen saw what was wrong with all such unrealistic novels, and cheerfully parodied them. When she set out to write her own she knew what not to do.

In *Sanditon*, the foolish Sir Edward disdains novels he calls "vapid tissues of ordinary occurrences from which no useful deductions can be drawn," but he condemns himself with those words, for Jane Austen makes of ordinary occurrences the highest art, the most moving and amusing drama. Her delineation of perception and motive are supreme and her dialogue is unsurpassed. Henry Austen quotes a review by Maria Jewsbury that pinpoints an important element of her novels: "The secret is, Miss Austen was a thorough mistress in the knowledge of human character; how it is acted upon by education and circumstance; and how, when once formed, it shows itself through every hour of every day, and in every speech to every person." But this knowledge of character would not make Austen's novels great if she did not also have consummate skill with the language. The narrative subtly moves in and out of the minds of the characters, showing objective and subjective realities, and the blending of the two. Conversations capture all the things people are doing when they speak besides conveying information. The narration is sophisticated and complex yet perfectly easy and natural. The comedy, whether witty or nonsensical, is unsurpassed, and delights the reader just as much upon the tenth reading as the first.

One could go on and on trying to describe all the perfections of Jane Austen's novels, but perhaps it is best to return again to the narrator's defense of novels in *Northanger Abbey* and simply leave it at that. Although Austen was defending the novels of others, the passage describes none of them as well as it describes her own novels, works in which "the greatest powers of the mind are displayed, in which the most thorough knowledge of human nature, the happiest delineation of its varieties, the liveliest effusions of wit and humour are conveyed to the world in the best chosen language."

101 WINCHESTER CATHEDRAL

Jane Austen was buried in Winchester Cathedral on July 24, 1817. The inscription on her tomb speaks of "the benevolence of her heart, the sweetness of her temper, and the extraordinary endowments of her mind" and of her "charity, devotion, faith and purity," but makes no mention of her being an author. In 1872, an additional plaque was placed in the cathedral, and that one does mention her writing. In the 1850s people would come to Winchester Cathedral on pilgrimages to Austen's grave. She was still so little known at that time, her nephew tells us, that the verger (the sacristan and caretaker) didn't know why they were interested and asked if "there was anything particular about that lady." Knowledge of "that lady" and the brilliant, unforgettable ladies and gentlemen she created has certainly spread since then. Jane Austen is surely, and deservedly, the world's favorite novelist.

References

I am deeply grateful for the work of these wonderful writers, scholars, editors, and publishers, which provided me invaluable resources.

Austen, Caroline. *My Aunt Jane Austen: A Memoir*. Written in 1867 and published by the Jane Austen Society in 1952.

Austen, Henry. "Biographical Notice of the Author." Preface to the first edition of *Northanger Abbey* and *Persuasion*, London, 1818. Revised version, preface to the 1833 edition of *Sense and Sensibility*, published by Richard Bentley.

Austen, Jane. *Emma*. London, 1816. Penguin Classics edition, edited and with an introduction by Ronald Blythe. Harmondsworth, UK: 1985. Quoted excerpts are from the 1985 edition.

———. *Lady Susan*. London, 1871. Penguin English Library edition, edited and with an introduction by Margaret Drabble. Harmondsworth, UK: 1975. Quoted excerpts are from the 1975 edition.

———. *Mansfield Park*. London, 1814. Penguin Classics edition, edited and with an introduction by Tony Tanner. Harmondsworth, UK: 1985. Quoted excerpts are from the 1985 edition.

————. *Northanger Abbey*. London, 1818. Penguin Classics edition, edited and with an introduction by Anne Ehrenpreis. Harmondsworth, UK: 1985. Quoted excerpts are from the 1985 edition.

————. "Opinions of *Mansfield Park*." In *Mansfield Park*, edited by Claudia L. Johnson, 375–378. New York: W. W. Norton, 1998.

————. *Persuasion*. London, 1818. Penguin Classics edition, edited and with an introduction by D. W. Harding. Harmondsworth, UK: 1965. Quoted excerpts are from the 1965 edition.

————. "Plan of A Novel." In *Emma*, edited by Stephen M. Parrish, 340–41. New York: W. W. Norton, 1993. Text based on *The Oxford Illustrated Jane Austen*, Vol. 6: *Minor Works*, edited by R. W. Chapman. London: Oxford University Press, 1954.

————. *Pride and Prejudice*. London, 1813. Norton Critical Edition, edited by Donald Gray. New York: W. W. Norton, 1993. Quoted excerpts are from the 1993 edition.

————. *Sanditon*. Penguin English Library edition, edited and with an introduction by Margaret Drabble. Harmondsworth, UK: 1975. Quoted excerpts are from the 1975 edition. Text based on *The Oxford Illustrated Jane Austen*, Vol. 6: *Minor Works*, edited by R. W. Chapman. London: Oxford University Press, 1954.

———. *Sense and Sensibility*. London, 1811. Penguin Classics edition, edited and with an introduction by Tony Tanner. Harmondsworth, UK: 1986. Quoted excerpts are from the 1986 edition.

———. *The Watsons*. London, 1871. First published in James-Edward Austen-Leigh's *A Memoir of Jane Austen*, 2nd ed. Penguin English Library edition, edited and with an introduction by Margaret Drabble. Harmondsworth, UK: 1975. Quoted excerpts are from the 1975 edition.

———. Juvenilia. Quotations from *Love and Freindship*, *Lesley Castle*, and *Jack & Alice* are from e-texts on Henry Churchyard's Jane Austen Information Page at *www.pemberley.com/janeinfo*. This site was also the source for e-texts of *Frederic & Elfrida* and *The Three Sisters*. (This site is a wonderful resource for texts and all kinds of information about Austen.)

———. *Jane Austen's Letters*. 3rd edition, edited by Deirdre Le Faye. Oxford: Oxford University Press, 1995. Quotations from Jane Austen's letters are from this edition.

Austen-Leigh, James-Edward. *A Memoir of Jane Austen*. 2nd ed. London, 1871. Quotations from the memoirs of James-Edward Austen-Leigh; Caroline Austen; Henry Austen; Anna Lefroy; and Fanny Lefroy; Fanny Knight's letter to her sister Marianne; and Catherine Hubback's letter to James-Edward Austen-Leigh are from *A Memoir of Jane Austen* and *Other Family Recollections*, edited by Kathryn Sutherland.

New York: Oxford University Press, 2002. The excerpt from Fanny Knight's letter in this book is taken from *Fanny Knight's Diaries: Jane Austen through her Niece's Eyes*, edited by Deirdre Le Faye, 38–39. Alton, U.K.: Jane Austen Society, 2000.

Cope, Sir Zachary. "Jane Austen's End." *British Medical Journal*. July 18, 1964, 182–83. Response by F. A. Bevan printed August 8, 1964, 394.

Dring, Melissa. "A New Portrait of Jane Austen." *Jane Austen's Regency World* 1 (2003): 5–9.

Hannon, Patrice. *Dear Jane Austen: A Heroine's Guide to Life and Love*. Coeur d'Alene, ID: Wytherngate Press, 2005.

Honan, Park. *Jane Austen: Her Life*. New York: St. Martin's Press 1987.

Lefroy, Anna. "Recollections of Aunt Jane." 1864.

Nicolson, Nigel. "Was Jane Austen Happy in Bath?" Lecture given at the Holburne Museum of Art, Bath, June 27, 2002.

Proudman, Elizabeth. "The Essential Guide to Finding Jane Austen in Chawton." Publication of the Jane Austen Society of North America, 2003.

Ratcliffe, Edward. "Transports of Delight: How Jane Austen's Characters Got Around." *The Inkwell*. Online publication of the Jane

Austen Society of North America, Northern California Region (*www
.jasnanorcal.org*), 2002.

Spence, Jon. "Mrs. Austen's Letter from Stoneleigh Abbey." Jane Austen Society of Australia Web site (*www.jasa.net.au*), January 13, 2004. Source for quotation from Mrs. Austen's letter.

Tomalin, Claire. *Jane Austen: A Life*. New York: Random House, 1999).

Index